The
9 AND 12
WORKBOOK

Don Carroll

ISBN: 0982926545
ISBN-13: 978-0-9829265-4-3

This Workbook and my Recovery belongs to:_____

TABLE OF CONTENTS

DEDICATION

This book is dedicated to my colleague Jane Strong whose commitment to the Ennegram and the insight and vitality it brings to 12 Step recoveries has led us to teach together and be formed by the synergy of these powerful strategies for renewal, creativity and spiritual growth.

ACKNOWLEDGMENTS

Helen Palmer is a spiritual pioneer in the landscape of the Enneagram. I owe her a special thanks for her encouragement, suggestions and review of a draft of this book. I am in debt to Robynn Moraites, Director of the North Carolina Lawyer Assistance Program and to all the workshop and retreat participants whose sharing of their experience of the power of the Enneagram in strengthening and maintaining their recoveries has been an inspiration which has helped compel the completion of this book. Special thanks also to Anne Vance and Brian Coon for their leadership in introducing the Enneagram as a tool in helping their extended care patients at the Pavillon Treatment Center in Mills Springs, North Carolina; and, to Tom Northern, Bev Barnes, and Susan Hickerson and the other able clinicians there who have understood its potential for insight, change and healing.

Preface

Tripping over Joy

What is the difference
Between your experience of Existence
And that of a saint?

The saint knows
That the spiritual path
Is a sublime chess game with God

And that the Beloved
Has just made such a Fantastic Move

That the saint is now continually
Tripping over Joy
And bursting out in Laughter
And saying, I surrender!

Whereas, my dear,
I'm afraid you still think

You have a thousand serious moves.

Hafiz

Set Aside Prayer

God, please help me set aside everything I think I know about myself, my disease, these Steps and especially You; For an open mind and a new experience with myself, my disease, these Steps and especially You. Amen.

Part I
Introduction to the Enneagram 12 Step Connection

Introduction

We all have a false-self, an ego self, which we construct in order to navigate the world. While developmentally it is necessary to construct a false-self. It in turn becomes a barrier to our authentic experience of life.

Addiction creates additional layers of false-self—protections against seeing clearly what is happening. We could say it super-sizes the false-self.

The Steps provide the means to deconstruct the false-self. Often in the first round of doing the Steps, the false-self is diminished enough for us to consolidate a good initial sobriety. But we are often left with enough residue of the false-self that we do not live lives that are happy, joyous and free.

Complete recovery and all spiritual growth is about moving through the remaining residue of the false-self.

How to Use this Workbook

One of the underlying principles of the Enneagram is that we each have a spark of divine essence. The spark of our divinity is like light. Light is composed of different bands of color. From different sources light reflects different shades of color. Yet each spark, or ray of light, contains all colors. Similarly, we each have a spark of divine essence that reflects particularly one of the nine aspects of the divine light of our humanity, and yet we also contain all aspects of the light of human divinity. Our individual spark of essence, or true self as it is sometimes described, is particularly associated with one of the nine Enneagram types.

The knowledge gained from understanding how we block being in our essence is jarring. We realize, maybe for the first time, that we have been in a trance most of our lives, unaware of what was driving our behavior, just as we have often been unaware of what drove our drinking and using. Because of the power of our ego-driven false-self, we can get sleepy, confused, doubtful, frightened or unconsciously develop some other strategy by which our ego prevents us from learning how to dismantle the trance in which our ego strategies put us.

As we learn about the Enneagram we must learn to recognize these kinds of feelings and patterns of thinking, and when they occur realize we have the opportunity to learn something particularly important. We must stay present and attentive in that moment for the learning to land. One of the best ways to approach this material is with genuine curiosity and open-mindedness. When we feel our curiosity going away, we are probably getting pulled back into our trance.

We know that we learn best when we are upbeat and not resistant to material being presented. We will get the most out of this workbook by approaching it in this positive fashion. We are simply learning how to return to our most authentic self. The good news is this material is not about teaching us something that we don't already have. Rather it is about building our awareness so that we can access what we may have lost touch with years ago, but which is already there—the precious essence of who we are.

So our approach to how we use this workbook is important. There is good reason to believe that the Enneagram has been around for centuries, but during this time its use has been only within esoteric spiritual traditions. It is possible that the reason for this was the belief that the knowledge the Enneagram provides is so powerful that it should only be provided to people inside of a spiritual discipline where each initiate has a spiritual guide to assist him or her in understanding and applying this knowledge. We are lucky this material is now available, but this doesn't lessen our need for guidance. Be sure to ask questions and seek guidance from others who deeply understand the Enneagram in recovery.

Origins of the Enneagram

We may be wondering—"why have I not heard, prior to this workshop, about the Enneagram?" There is a good reason. While the template the Enneagram provides has been used for many years in esoteric spiritual traditions, it has only recently come to be written and talked about publicly. In the Western Christian tradition, we trace the origins of the Enneagram through the sands of time at least as far back as the Desert Fathers and Mothers.

One of the great Desert Fathers was Evagrius Ponticus. Evagrius was born in 345 A.D. in an area south of Russia in what is modern-day Georgia. He studied in Constantinople and Jerusalem before becoming a monk in Egypt, where he lived in the desert and wrote several books we still have today. Evagrius was greatly influenced by Pythagoras.

The work of Evagrius coincides with the Enneagram in two important ways: the symbol of the Enneagram itself is an image based on Pythagorean numerology and his writing reflects an Enneagram understanding of the psychology of human nature.

In Evagrius' book, *Teachings on the Passions*, Evagrius develops a list of eight, or in one reference he notes nine, vices, or distracting emotions or thoughts that impede the way to God and serenity. His list of eight passions or vices in his *Teachings on the Passions* is: anger (One in the Enneagram), pride (Two), vanity or thirst for glory (Three), sadness in the sense of self-pity or envy (Four), avarice (Five), gluttony (Seven), lust (Eight) and laziness or torpor (Nine). Fear which is identified with type Six in the Enneagram may be understood as the passion, or emotional vice, from which all other passions flow. Later, Pope Gregory the First reduced the list to the one we know today as the Seven Deadly Sins consisting of: anger, pride, envy, greed, gluttony, lust, and sloth. While Evagrius did not systematize the nine points of the Enneagram as we know them today he came extraordinarily close.

The second thing that Evagrius did was elucidate the symbolic meaning of the Enneagram as a symbol of the order and dynamics of the cosmos. This came from his interest and understanding of Pythagorean mathematics. He started from the story told at the end of the Gospel of John after Jesus' resurrection, where Jesus ordered his disciples to cast their fishing nets into the sea. They obeyed and caught 153 fish. Evagrius developed an interpretation of the symbolic meaning of catching 153 fish. His explanation is found in his book, *153 Chapters on Prayer*. In that book Evagrius writes:

> *I have divided this treatise on prayer into 153 chapters. With them I am sending you a tidbit of the Gospel, so that you can rejoice in a symbolic number that joins together a triangular and a hexagonal figure. The triangle stands symbolically for the Trinity, the hexagon for the orderly creation of the world in six days. The number 100 describes a square, the number 53 a triangle and at the same time a circle. Why? Because it is the sum of 25 and 28. 28 is a triangle and 25 is the square, since 25 is 5 times 5. Thus this sum represents a square figure since it represents the four-fold qualities of the seven virtues. Through its round form the circle expresses the river of time and is simultaneously an appropriate symbol for true knowledge of the world. In the river of time week follows week, month follows month, year follows year, and season follows season, as the movement of the sun and moon, spring and summer, etc., show. The triangle, which is expressed in the number 28, stands for knowledge of the holy Trinity. Or we could*

interpret the entire sum of 153 as a triangle referring to ascetical practice, the contemplation of nature, and the meditation on the spiritual knowledge of God -- or faith, hope, and love, or gold, silver, and precious stones. So much on this number.

According to Evagrius the triangle stands for the divine nature of reality, the hexagon for the created world and the circle for the course of time and true knowledge. There are many ways to graphically represent together the triangle, hexagon and circle. The modern figure that we have of the Enneagram, as set out below, is one of those ways.

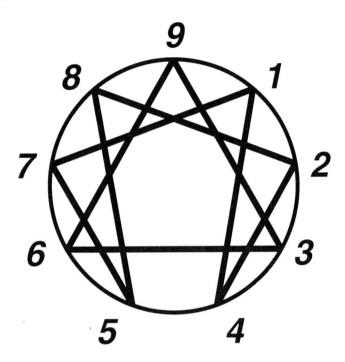

What is so profoundly stunning about Evagrius' work is that it includes both a psychology of human character based on eight (or in one case he says nine) energy systems in the body which deter the evolution of consciousness and a mathematically driven symbolic image combining a circle, square and hexagon representing the universe.

There is also evidence of the Enneagram's use within the Christian monastic tradition over the centuries. For example, the ideas of the Enneagram are seen in the work of Ramon Lull who grew up on the island of Marjorca in the 1200s. When he was 27 years old, in 1263, he had a profound conversion experience. After that he became a member of the Third Order of the Franciscans which is open to married people.

Lull was very interested in converting others to Christianity and in having serious religious dialogue with Jews and Muslims. He believed that there was a common language of spirituality which could bring people together and reduce conflict in the world. Lull thought that the starting point for advancing this common language of spirituality was in identifying nine qualities of God, which he distributed around a circular figure. Lull's figure also included a triangle. The closeness of his image to that of Evagrius' figure and to the modern image of the Enneagram is unmistakable. Lull represented the qualities of God as a tree of life just as the Kabbalah does. In addition to the closeness of his ideas to mystical Judaism, he saw a connection of his ideas to mystical Islam, particularly Sufism. Both Teresa of Avila and John of the Cross were students of Lull's, suggesting a perpetuation of Enneagram learning within the flowering of the mystical Christian community during the Middle Ages.

The Enneagram was publicly introduced at the beginning of the 20th century by George Ivanovich Gurdjieff. Gurdjieff presented the Enneagram as a symbol of the dynamic structure of the cosmos. From this dynamic structure Gurdjieff developed a series of movements that were designed to reflect the Enneagram's structure and allow his students to develop greater awareness and consciousness to break free of patterns which repeatedly took them down the same track of their false-self trance.

Thus, Gurdjieff presented the Enneagram as a direct path to greater consciousness, without including in it an understanding of ego structure. Gurdjieff's sources for his knowledge of the Enneagram are unclear but a common assumption is that he learned about the Enneagram from the Sufis in Asia.

The Origins of Alcoholics Anonymous

The Oxford Group was a Christian organization founded by an American Christian missionary, Dr. Frank Buchman. Its ideas touched a chord in the zeitgeist of the 1920s and 1930s and it grew rapidly in the 1930s. It is credited with helping sow a spirit of resolve among movements in Norway and Denmark that kept the resistance alive after the invasion of the Nazis. The Oxford Group was not a religion but a template for being living Christianity. One of the organization's key leaders in the United States was Sam Shoemaker.

Both of the founders of AA attended meetings of the Oxford Group and were exposed to its teaching before the Twelve Steps were formulated and the *Big Book* was written. Harvey Firestone had invited Buchman to Akron in 1933 and this resulted in the founding of an Oxford Group there whose members included Bob and Ann Smith.

Roland Hazard had famously gone to see Carl Jung in Switzerland to try to find a cure for his alcoholism and been told by Dr. Jung that his condition was hopeless absent a psyche altering spiritual experience. Hazard then sought to find a way to have a spiritual experience by joining an Oxford Group. Along the way Hazard met Ebby Thacher, another alcoholic, and introduced him to the Oxford group. For awhile Thacher lived at the Calvary Rescue Mission run by Sam Shoemaker who taught the concept of God being of one's understanding to the drunks the mission catered to. In keeping with the Oxford Group tradition of witnessing, Thacher went to visit Bill Wilson at his home where he introduced him to the Oxford Groups ideas for a "conversion cure" for his alcoholism.

As the story famously goes, Bill Wilson, an agnostic, was "aghast" when Thacher told him he had "got religion." A few days later in a drunken state Bill went to the Calvary Rescue Mission in search of Ebby. There he attended his first Oxford Group meeting. Days later he re-admitted himself to Townes Hospital for the fourth time, where in severe alcohol withdrawal he called out in desperation to God and had a profound spiritual experience, which began his journey of sobriety that would lead to the founding of AA with Dr. Bob Smith.

Sam Shoemaker and Bill Wilson developed a friendship. The Oxford Group had by this time a lot of literature. One historian has found that almost 200 words and phrases used by Shoemaker to describe the Oxford Group can be found in AA literature and language. The Oxford Group liked using short pithy slogans. Perhaps more importantly than specific words, many of the basic ideas in the *Big Book* and the Twelve Steps are found in Oxford Group literature. These include:

1. That connection with something outside ourselves (God) is essential for change within
2. That sin is a blockage of connection with God (the power outside ourselves)
3. That surrender is necessary to break the blockage
4. That public confession of sin is needed for the surrender to be owned
5. That spiritual growth is not one-stop, but must be continually nurtured by daily surrender and having quiet time with God
6. That fellowship and witnessing to others are necessary to continue to energize ongoing spiritual growth

All of these Oxford Group ideas are reflected in the Twelve Steps of AA. Similarly many of these ideas are reflected in the ideas of authors writing about the Enneagram. These include:

1. That spiritual growth is the key to the resolution of most of what seem like intractable psychological issues that people have; or, as the Buddhist would say, the problem of suffering.

2. That the Enneagram provides an individualized map for each of us to understand what are the blocks—the unconsciously operating pattern of our type structure--that prevent our spiritual growth.

3. That through various spiritual practices, including meditation, we can become aware of when we are triggered by our false-self type pattern and through the development of a witnessing inner observer learn to be at choice about whether that pattern operates.

4. As we become more at choice, and the constriction of the contraction of our false-self loosens, many of the psychological issues in our lives fall away and we become more free, present and joyful.

5. Ongoing spiritual practice and development are necessary because otherwise the unconscious pattern, being of course unconscious and out of awareness and survival driven, will reassert itself.

6. The Enneagram in the Narrative Tradition promotes the use of panels in which participants are given the opportunity to speak publicly about their blocks. The witnessing process of the Narrative Tradition provides a living teaching tool about type and also a therapeutic process for individuals to explore their unique experiences of how their lives are affected by the blocks of their type.

There is a connection between the Enneagram as presented by Gurdjieff and the development of the Twelve Steps. One of Gurdjieff's earliest students was Maurice Nicoll. Nicoll was born in England and trained there as a physician. He then went to Zurich where he studied directly with Carl Jung whose teachings awoke in him an interest in the spiritual nature of healing. After that he met P. D. Ouspensky, who introduced him to the work of Gurdjieff. Nicoll then went to France and trained for a year in Gurdjieff's program of consciousness evolution. Later he became a teacher and writer about the Gurdjieff system which was known as the Fourth Way. During the 1930s and 1940s Fourth Way groups and the writings of Nicoll became prominent in circles of spiritual seekers in New York and other major cities in the United States.

We know that Bill Wilson was a spiritual seeker and it is likely he knew participants in the Fourth Way. Some believe his *Big Book* references in his own story (p.8) and in Chapter Two, There is a Solution, (p.25) of being "rocketed into a fourth dimension" was an illusion to the Fourth Way. He was assisted in the writing of the *Twelve Steps and Twelve Traditions* by Thomas E. Powers another recovering alcoholic. In the Tenth Step section of the *Twelve Steps and Twelve Traditions*, there is discussion of the need for a "spot-check inventory taken in the midst of such disturbances" as anger, envy, pride, etc (i.e the underlying emotional triggers of Enneagram types). The spot check inventory is, in addict-friendly language, what in Enneagram terms is called the development of the inner observer, that is our inner capacity to observe our own process of reactivity to life. The passage in the *Twelve Steps and Twelve Traditions* reflects Thomas E. Powers knowledge of Nicoll's writings. In Nicoll's later book, *Invitation to a Great Experiment*, he uses the term watching for this process of inner observation and says:

> The practice of watching plays a prominent part in the psychology of Ouspensky and Gurdjieff, where it is broken down into two disciplines: 1) self observation and 2) self-remembering. The former is a way of watching oneself as an objective person. The latter is a technique of touching a higher level within oneself. Both work together toward awakening from spiritual sleep.

The Common Idea of a Spiritual Solution

In the 1970s, a Chilean named Oscar Ichazo publicly developed a model of the Enneagram based upon Gurdjieff's work and other veiled sources. Claudio Naranjo became a student of Ichazo and fostered a community at Esalen at Big Sur in California, that focused on using the Enneagram as a method for the evolution of consciousness. Evolution of consciousness became the "neutral" language to describe the goal of spiritual transformation that would allow us to drop the masks of our false-self.

Among those who first heard Naranjo's ideas was Helen Plamer, who would later establish the Enneagram in the Narrative Tradition with Dr. David Daniels. Another early student of Naranjo's was Robert Ochs, a Jesuit, who taught at Loyola. Through Och's teachings numerous Jesuits began to speak and write publicly about the Enneagram and use it openly in providing spiritual guidance. Most of the early books written about the Enneagram were authored by members of religious orders. In short, the Enneagram attracted the attention of the same sort of spiritual pioneers as those who were involved in the Oxford Group a generation earlier. The Oxford Group, with its tools for spiritual growth, provided the spiritual cornerstone on which Alcoholics Anonymous is based. The Enneagram template focuses these ideas more sharply. Enneagram spiritual writers, the Oxford Group ideas and the Twelve Steps of AA, all use common ideas to explore a path of spiritual transformation.

THE AA TREE OF SPIRITUAL TRANSFORMATION

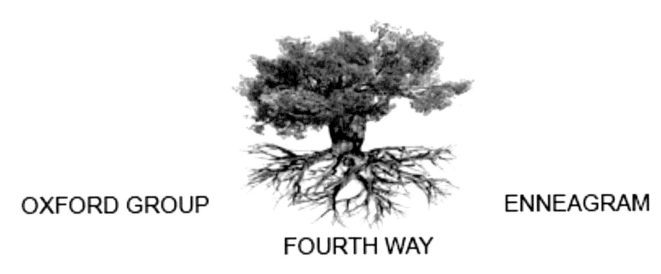

OXFORD GROUP   ENNEAGRAM

FOURTH WAY

The AA tree of spiritual transformation has many roots.

*   *   *

The modern version of the Enneagram with the names often given to the nine different personality types to reflect their different ways of thinking, feeling and doing is provided here.

NINE WAYS OF FEELING, THINKING AND DOING

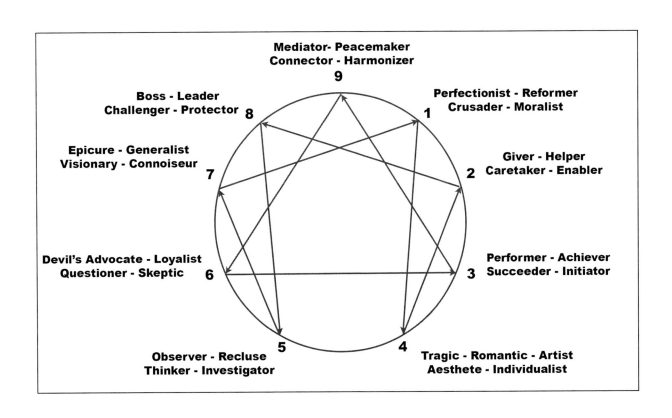

Interconnections between the Enneagram and the Twelve Steps

The first interconnection between the Enneagram and the Twelve Steps is readily apparent. We see that the image of AA, a triangle within a circle, is an integral part of the Enneagram image.

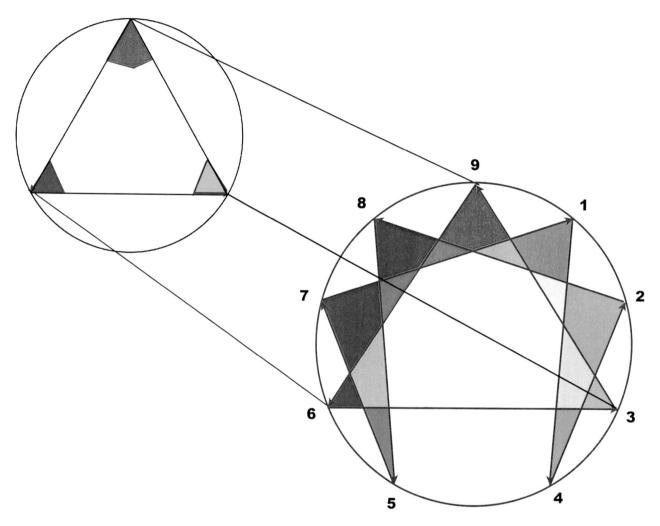

Bill Wilson is said to have arrived at the image of the AA symbol in a dream. The dream image could have come from his seeing the Enneagram image in exposure to Gurdjieff's work. Perhaps its origin is simply from the archetypal nature of the Enneagram, or as Jung would say from our collective unconscious. The three points of the AA symbol stand for unity, service and recovery. These correspond to the three Enneagram points of the central triangle: point Nine, the higher aspect of which is often described as unity; point Three, the higher aspect of which conveys the idea of glorious service without ego attachment; and point Six, which has the higher aspect of quiet mind and awake-ness, a state of being that can readily be equated to recovery in full bloom.

We next see that there are many additional ways that the Enneagram neatly fits into the Steps. For example, Step 10 on page 86 of the *Big Book* tells us how to take a nightly inventory. It lists each of the nine aspects of the false-self that block us from being in the essence of the respective Enneagram types. This will be explored in more detail on page 85.

We also see that the *Twelve and Twelve* refers directly to the Seven Deadly Sins as a way to understand our character defects. "To avoid falling into confusion over the names these defects should be called, let's take a universally recognized list of major human failings—the Seven Deadly Sins of pride, greed, lust, anger, gluttony, envy and sloth." (p.48, *Twelve Steps and Twelve Traditions*) In addition, there are many references throughout the Big Book and the Twelve and Twelve which refer to fear and self dishonesty (the two blocks missing from the Seven Deadly Sins) as the key drivers undermining our ability to live more spiritual lives.

Let's compare the spiritual promises of AA with the spiritual transformation that the Enneagram promises.

The *Big Book* of AA says:

"We are going to know a new freedom and a new happiness. We will not regret the past nor wish to shut the door on it. We will comprehend the word serenity and we will know peace. No matter how far down the scale we have gone, we will see how our experience can benefit others. That feeling of uselessness and self pity will disappear. We will lose interest in selfish things and gain interest in our fellows. Self-seeking will slip away. Our whole attitude and outlook upon life will change. Fear of people and of economic insecurity will leave us. We will intuitively know how to handle situations which used to baffle us. We will suddenly realize that God is doing for us what we could not do for ourselves."

- Promises of AA, from the *Big Book*

What many people don't realize is that upon close examination we see the promises of AA explicitly include a promise directed to each of the Enneagram's nine types.

"We are going to know a new freedom and a new happiness. (7)
We will not regret the past nor wish to shut the door on it. (4)
We will comprehend the word serenity and we will know peace. (9)
No matter how far down the scale we have gone, we will see how our experience can benefit others. (2)
That feeling of uselessness and self pity will disappear. (1)
We will lose interest in selfish things and gain interest in our fellows. (5)

Self-seeking will slip away. (3)
Our whole attitude and outlook upon life will change. (All)
Fear of people and of economic insecurity will leave us. (6)
We will intuitively know how to handle situations which used to baffle us. (All).
We will suddenly realize that God is doing for us what we could not do for ourselves." (8)

This gives us an Enneagram of the Promises of AA.

ENNEAGRAM OF THE PROMISES OF AA

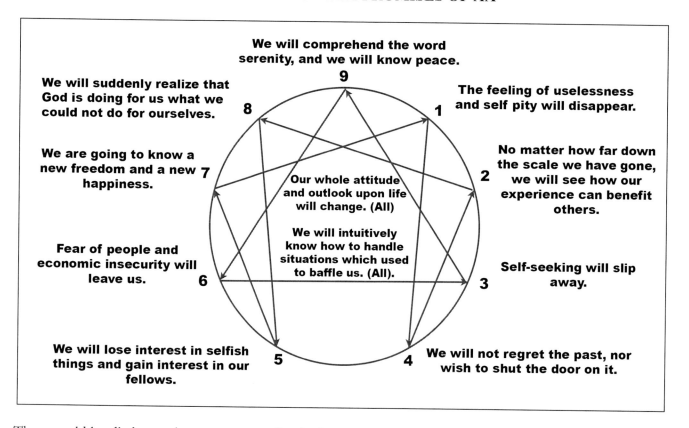

There could hardly be any better argument for the interconnecting reinforcement of using the Enneagram as a tool in our recoveries than the simple reality that the promises of AA point directly to what each type is like when each type is restored to its authentic essence.

<u>Why do we want to be in our Enneagram essence?</u>

While it may seem the answer to this is obvious, it is an important question to ask ourselves. If we are going to use the knowledge the Enneagram offers, what does it lead to? What are the Promises of the Enneagram? Because it is a spiritual tool the Promises of the Enneagram are called the Holy Ideas. The Holy Idea for each type is that divine spark in the essence of each type.

The promise of living from essence is that we will actually live the qualities of the Enneagram's Holy Ideas. Living from the essence of our type means we embody the type's virtue.

<u>TYPE</u>	<u>Holy Idea</u>	<u>Virtue</u>
Type 1	Holy Perfection	Serenity
Type 2	Holy Will	Humility
Type 3	Holy Hope	Honesty
Type 4	Holy Origin	Equanimity
Type 5	Holy Omniscience	Non-attachment
Type 6	Holy Faith	Courage
Type 7	Holy Plan	Sobriety
Type 8	Holy Truth	Innocence
Type 9	Holy Love	Right action

This is how it looks in Enneagram form.

Enneagram of Holy Ideas and Virtues

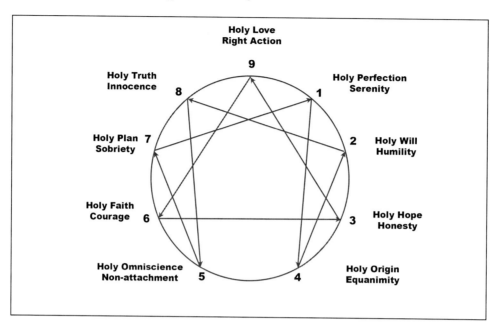

The promises of AA and the promised gifts of the Enneagram reflect the spiritual gifts promised in other spiritual traditions.

For example, in the Christian tradition we find, not surprisingly, that there are nine gifts of the Spirit that correspond to the nine different types of the Enneagram. Galatians 5:22 reads:

"But the fruit of the Spirit is love, joy, peace, long-suffering, gentleness, goodness, faith, meekness, temperance."

This translates into the Enneagram of the Fruit of the Spirit.

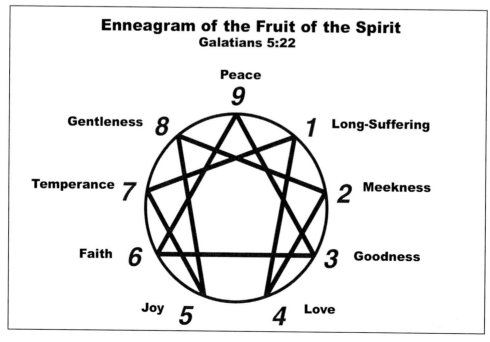

In Buddhism, four states of being are called the four immeasurables because there is no limitations to their depth or scope. Unlike reactive emotions, the four immeasurables do not function in the service of any habituated pattern, sense of self or personal agenda. They are equanimity, loving-kindness, compassion and joy.

Incorporating knowledge of the Enneagram into our recovery lives offers to help us have exactly the same spiritual awakening that the Steps promise us. These are the same gifts promised by the great spiritual traditions. Using both the Enneagram and the Steps together provides one of the most powerful processes for spiritual awakening that exists today in our modern world.

Here is an image which combines the Promises of AA by type with the virtue of each type. Notice how closely they align.

ENNEAGRAM OF THE PROMISES OF AA
AND VIRTUES

We will comprehend the word
serenity, and we will know peace.
Right Action
9

The feeling of uselessness
and self pity will disappear.
Serenity

We will suddenly realize that
God is doing for us what we
could not do for ourselves.
Innocence
8

1

No matter how far down
the scale we have gone,
we will see how our
experience can benefit
others.
Humility
2

We are going to know a
new freedom and a new
happiness.
Sobriety
7

Our whole attitude
and outlook upon life
will change. (All)

We will intuitively
know how to handle
situations which used
to baffle us. (All).

Self-seeking will slip
away.
Honesty
3

Fear of people and
economic insecurity will
leave us.
Courage
6

We will lose interest in selfish
things and gain interest in our
fellows.
Non-Attachment
5

4
We will not regret the past, nor
wish to shut the door on it.
Equanimity

Energetics of Recovery

Recovery works when we put the energy of our dis-ease to work in service of our recovery. There is a lot of energy in being irritable, restless and discontent. There is a lot of energy in our compulsion to drink or to use. To recover we must turn our obsession with alcohol into an obsession with recovery, working the Steps and helping others.

The Enneagram gives us a map to understand our energy, both how we squander our energy and how we can use it for our spiritual growth. Using the Enneagram for transformation we use the energy of our compulsive self to energize our awareness, to keep us present so that the false-self does not have the energy to run its program. We use the energy of our compulsion to keep us present and curious, rather than repressing or acting out the energy which defines and drives our false-self type. We then gradually become more naturally grounded in our essence. Then the Promises of AA and the Enneagram begin to come true.

The Enneagram Map Points Us to Home—to Who We Are in Wholeness

Often times a sponsor will ask a sponsee working on Step Two to write out a vision of sanity. If you are hoping to be restored to sanity, it is good to know what you are aiming for. Using the map the Enneagram provides, which points each of us toward our essence, adds additional meaning to this process. By knowing the Holy Idea and Virtue of our type we know what we are seeking to re-ground ourselves in by the surrendering we do in the Steps. The journey becomes a bit lighter when we can clearly see the destination.

Part II
Preparing to Take the Steps
Using the Enneagram

THE HOLY IDEAS

One of the basic underlying principles of the Enneagram is that each person comes into the world with an aspect of divinity. There are nine different aspects to this spark of divinity. When we are in our essence we live in the energy of our essential spark. These nine essence sparks are known as the Holy Ideas, or the points of wholeness for each of the nine types. Following is a description of each of these Holy Ideas or Energies of Wholeness.

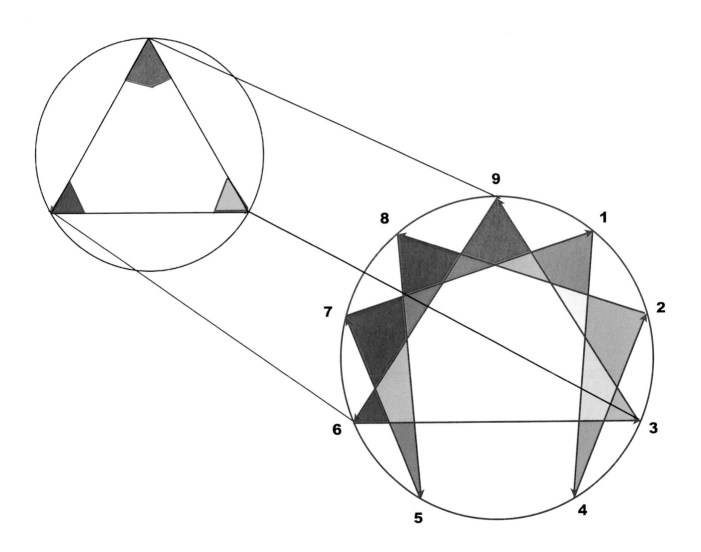

ENNEAGRAM POINT ONE

Point One – The Noble Guide of Holy Perfection

The Holy Idea is Holy Perfection, the recognition that Reality is inherently perfect, and we are part of that reality, so the purpose of working on ourselves cannot be to try to become better or to make our lives better, rather it is to embrace all of us, to be whole. A quality of impeccability, serenity and wisdom.

When we are in Type One wholeness we have integrity, wisdom, and self-discipline. We are fair, organized and ethical.

What Ones tell us when their drinking/using "was working":

"We drank to quiet the critical voices in our head."

"We drank not to feel so self critical all the time."

"We drank not to be so resentful."

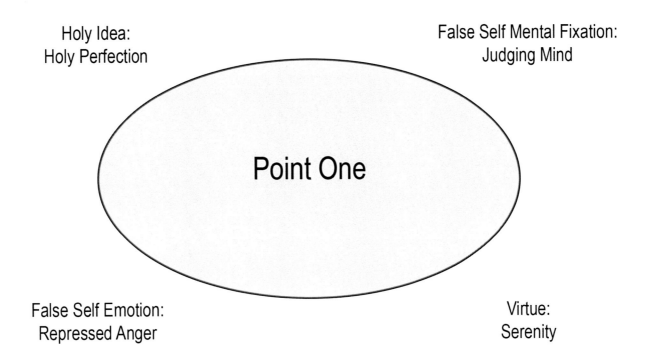

Holy Idea:
Holy Perfection

False Self Mental Fixation:
Judging Mind

Point One

False Self Emotion:
Repressed Anger

Virtue:
Serenity

Exercise for Type One

When my drinking/using "was working" I drank/used because:

_____

_____

_____

_____

_____

_____

_____

_____

_____

_____

_____

_____

_____

_____

_____

_____

_____

The false-self of the Type One tries to imitate the real essence quality: The ego wants to control goodness, to do that it needs to create a sense of superiority in order to feel there is control. It gets stuck in the polarity of what is good. Being right gives a false sense of being real.

The false-self of the One can pan for the gold of perfection over and over.

Basic False-Self Proposition: There is a right way and a wrong way to do everything.

Habitual False-Self Focus of Attention: What is right or wrong, correct or incorrect.

What Ones tell us about themselves when they are in their false-self compulsion:

"We live with a powerful inner critic that monitors every thought, word, and deed."

"We worry about getting things right and are unusually sensitive to criticism."

"We strive for perfection and feel responsible."

"We focus on being good and repress our impulses/desires for pleasures."

"We can be rigid, overly controlled, seeing virtue as its own reward."

The false-self uses our mental energy and our emotional energy to compulsively run its ego program.

<u>Exercise</u>

What have I learned about how the false-self of Type One keeps me in my ego trance?

_____

_____

_____

_____

_____

_____

_____

_____

_____

_____

_____

_____

_____

_____

_____

_____

_____

_____

_____

_____

_____

_____

_____

_____

_____

_____

_____

_____

ENNEAGRAM POINT TWO

Point Two – The Humble Healer & Graceful Giver

The Holy Idea is Holy Freedom, the awareness that Reality flows with a certain force, and the easiest way to deal with this force is to move with it, and that at the center of this force is God's Will. A natural heart presence-ness.

When we are in Type Two wholeness we are kind, appreciative, and generous. We are helpful, encouraging and empathetic, and above all we reach out to others humbly.

ACT
WITHOUT
EXPECTATION

- Lao Tzu

What Twos tell us when their drinking/using "was working":

"We drank to feel emotionally connected."

"We drank because of our hurt feelings."

"We were oversensitive to what other people needed and life was too painful not to drink."

"We would drink so we felt comfortable going out and getting the attention we needed."

"We drank when we felt we were not needed."

"We drank to celebrate when the need to be needed was satisfied."

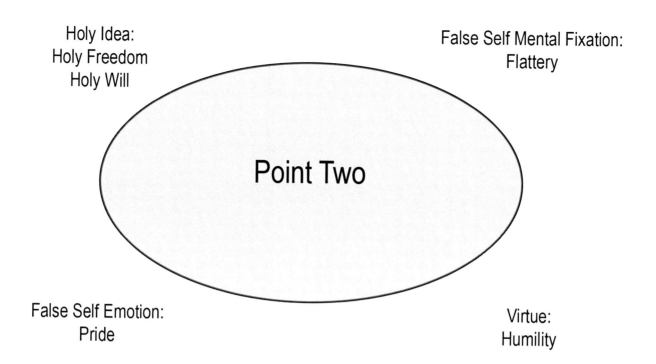

Holy Idea:
Holy Freedom
Holy Will

False Self Mental Fixation:
Flattery

Point Two

False Self Emotion:
Pride

Virtue:
Humility

Exercise for Type Two

When my drinking/using "was working" I drank/used because:

The false-self of the Type Two tries to imitate the real essence quality: Twos long for the heart connection of its essence and so the false-self tries to create this in order to feel loved. In the process it overlooks connecting with self. The irony is that without first connecting with self there is no way to really connect with another.

Basic False-Self Proposition: Love and survival depend on "giving to get."

Habitual False-Self Focus of Attention: Other people's needs.

What Twos tell us about themselves when they are in their false-self compulsion:

"We have a preoccupation with the needs of others."

"We have pride in giving and helping."

"We sometimes feel taken advantage of."

"We have a hard time expressing our own needs."

"We are manipulative."

"We alter our self-presentation to meet the needs of important others."

The false-self uses our mental energy and our emotional energy to compulsively run its ego program.

Depending on another
PERSON
for Your happiness
IS LIKE
Using Crutches
inspite of having
FEET

<u>Exercise</u>

What have I learned about how the false-self of Type Two keeps me in my ego trance?

ENNEAGRAM POINT THREE

Point Three – Dynamic Being of Glory

The Holy Idea is Holy Harmony, seeing that all experience is part of the great reality illuminated by the transcendent. From our being we glorify God. Abiding in a heart-felt appreciation for being.

When we are in Type Three wholeness we move in the world with an effortless energy of grace and flow. We are inspirational, productive, motivating and we glorify creation by our work.

its not my fault that when I was a baby I was dropped
in a box of GLITTER
and IVE BEEN shining ever since

What Threes tell us when their drinking/using "was working":

"We used to be more efficient."

"We drank because we worked all the time and it was the only way we could get a break."

"We drank to get in touch with ourselves."

"We drank to relax and forget about doing."

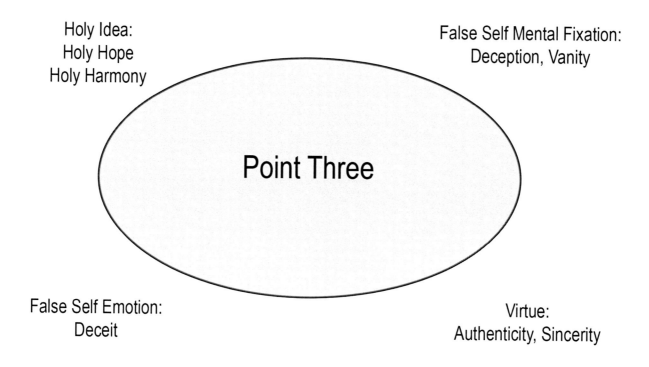

Holy Idea:
Holy Hope
Holy Harmony

False Self Mental Fixation:
Deception, Vanity

Point Three

False Self Emotion:
Deceit

Virtue:
Authenticity, Sincerity

Exercise for Type Three

When my drinking/using "was working" I drank/used because:

_____

_____

_____

_____

_____

_____

_____

_____

_____

_____

_____

_____

_____

_____

_____

The false-self of the Type Three tries to imitate the real essence quality: The Three tries to create glory. Tries to accomplish stuff so that it will have this feeling of being lit up by the accomplishment.

Basic False-Self Proposition:
Love and recognition are only for "champions".

Habitual False-Self Focus of Attention:
Tasks, Roles & Results

What Threes tell us about themselves when they are in their false-self compulsion:
"Our primary identification is with accomplishment and success."

"We seek approval and acceptance based on performance."

"Our attention goes to task."

"Our image is important."

"We feel constant pressure to perform."

"We lose attention to feelings: 'Not Now'."

"No one else is as efficient as I am."

To stop striving, we need only to fully realize that we are not separate doers, and spiritually surrender even though we may feel profound vulnerability, fragility, inadequacy, and weakness.

The false-self uses our mental energy and our emotional energy to compulsively run its ego program.

<u>Exercise</u>

What have I learned about how the false-self of Type Three keeps me in my ego trance?

ENNEAGRAM POINT FOUR

Point Four – The Bringer of Holy Beauty

The Holy Idea is Holy Origin, the perception and understanding that all appearance is nothing but the manifestation of Being; I am connected to Holy Origin and so is everyone and everything else. The real quality is knowing who I really am, an authentic sense of being without having to have my own original story.

When we are in Type Four wholeness we have depth, beauty and intimacy with life. We are authentic, creative and expressive in profound ways.

What Fours tell us when their drinking/using "was working":

"We drank to feel how special we are."

"We drank and used to experience our uniqueness."

"We drank because when we did for a while we didn't feel so depressed."

"We drank to forget our feelings of deficiency."

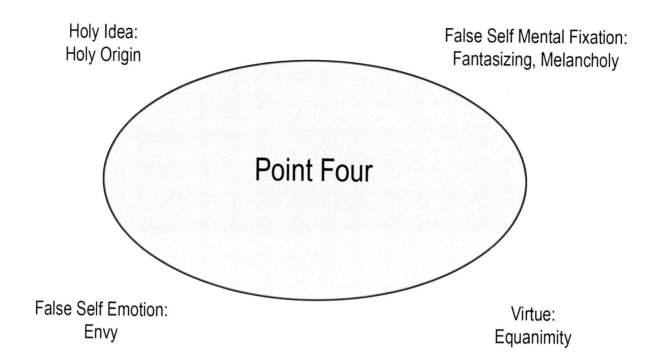

Holy Idea:
Holy Origin

False Self Mental Fixation:
Fantasizing, Melancholy

Point Four

False Self Emotion:
Envy

Virtue:
Equanimity

Exercise for the Type Four

When my drinking/using "was working" I drank/used because:

The false-self of the Type Four tries to imitate the real essence quality: The ego cannot bear the loss of the feeling of intimacy with being, so it creates fake intimacy, fake beauty, fake depth., some way to feel special. The desire for depth becomes the desire for the intensity of emotions. The talking about one's emotions becomes a block to experiencing them.

Basic False-Self Proposition: Others enjoy the happiness that I have been denied.

Habitual False-Self Focus of Attention: "Best" is what's missing.

What Fours tell us about themselves when they are in their false-self compulsion:

"We feel a constant longing for a missing ingredient for personal happiness."

"Our focus is on the best of what's missing, what's distant, and what's hard to get."

"For us the "ordinary" is painful."

"We experience a deeply felt abandonment that translates into a belief that "I am unlovable"."

"We feel special and elite. Our suffering sets us apart from others."

"Talking about one's emotions becomes a block to actually experiencing them."

The false-self uses our mental energy and our emotional energy to compulsively run its own ego program.

No one can make you feel inferior without your consent.

– Eleanor Roosevelt (1884-1962)

<u>Exercise</u>

What have I learned about how the false-self of Type Four keeps me in my ego trance?

ENNEAGRAM POINT FIVE

Point Five – The All Seeing Teacher

The Holy Idea is Holy Omniscience, which includes all that exists in its various manifestations, yet this diversity does not negate the fact of unity. A penetrating quality of being able to truly know.

When we are in Type Five wholeness we have clarity and direct knowing. We are curious, observing and able to see both the forest and the trees. We do not feel attached to "knowing it all."

What Fives tell us when their drinking/using "was working":

"We drank so life would not be such a drain on us."

"We drank and listened to music by ourselves and felt okay."

"We drank to escape into our minds."

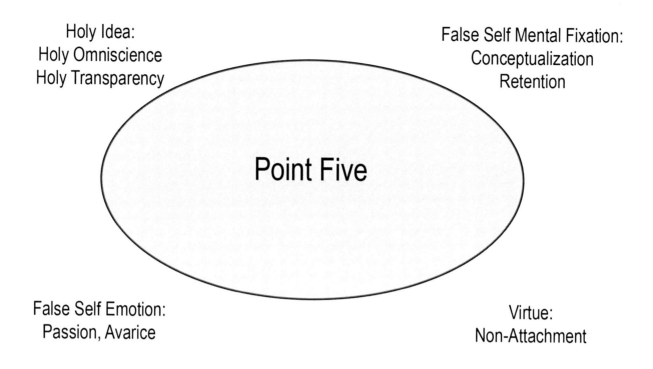

Holy Idea:
Holy Omniscience
Holy Transparency

False Self Mental Fixation:
Conceptualization
Retention

Point Five

False Self Emotion:
Passion, Avarice

Virtue:
Non-Attachment

Exercise for the Type Five

When my drinking/using "was working" I drank/used because:

The false-self of the Type Five tries to imitate the real essence quality: The ego retains information as a substitute for knowing truth. To feel okay one gets more and more facts. The false-self substitutes isolation for the need for inner quietness in the false hope that the real truth will be revealed by the isolation. The ego becomes more concerned with conserving resources (energy, time, feelings, money, etc.) than allowing life to unfold.

Basic False-Self Proposition: Love and respect are gained by practicing self-sufficiency.

Habitual False-Self Focus of Attention: What others want from me.

What Fives tell us about themselves when they are in their false-self compulsion:

"We have a marked need for privacy."

"We limit intrusion from a world that wants too much from us."

"We hoard time, space, energy, knowledge and ourselves."

"We detach from feelings and observe rather than participate."

The false-self uses our mental energy and our emotional energy to compulsively run its ego program.

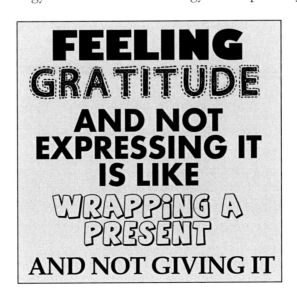

FEELING GRATITUDE AND NOT EXPRESSING IT IS LIKE WRAPPING A PRESENT AND NOT GIVING IT

<u>Exercise</u>

What have I learned about how the false-self of Type Five keeps me in my ego trance?

ENNEAGRAM POINT SIX

Point Six – The Courageous Hero of Faith

The Holy Idea is Holy Faith, a matter of realizing that Being is an inner reality and inner truth of every human being, that Being is a real presence, that it is intrinsically good, and that it is the way things are supposed to be. The capacity to be alive and awake to what is, to be fully present to life's journey.

When we are in Type Six wholeness we are awakened, present and trusting. We are trustworthy, committed, reliable and faithful.

What Sixes tell us when their drinking/using "was working":

"We drank to relax."

"We drank so we would not feel this anxiety and pressure all the time."

"We drank for the beauty of the feelings we would have at first."

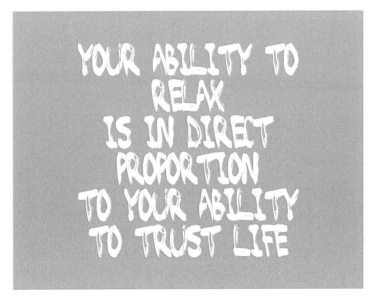

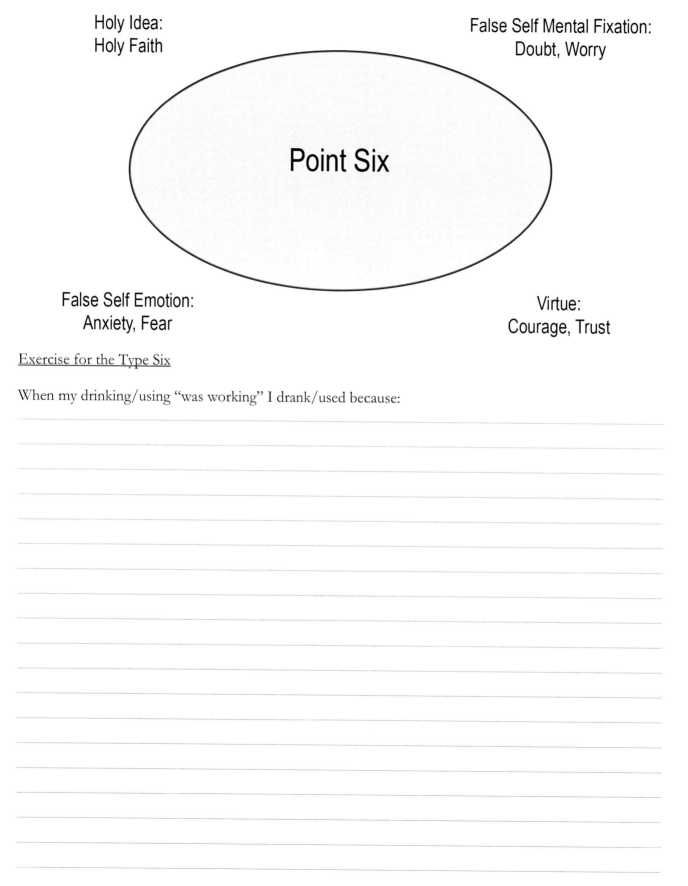

Holy Idea:
Holy Faith

False Self Mental Fixation:
Doubt, Worry

Point Six

False Self Emotion:
Anxiety, Fear

Virtue:
Courage, Trust

Exercise for the Type Six

When my drinking/using "was working" I drank/used because:

The false-self of the Type Six tries to imitate the real essence quality: Tries to create a sense of security so it can feel at home. The effort to create this sense of security actually blocks it. The ego tries to keep track of everything for security and because this is always impossible it creates more anxiety for the Six.

> "We're so busy watching out for what's just ahead of us that we don't take time to enjoy where we are."

— Calvin & Hobbs

Basic False-Self Proposition: Love and protection are gained by vigilance and endurance.

Habitual False-Self Focus of Attention: Threat, hazard, difficulties.

What Sixes tell us about themselves when they are in their false-self compulsion:

"We are preoccupied with safety and security concerns."

"We greet everything with a doubting mind, and contrary thinking."

"We have active imaginations that amplify questionable areas."

"We question people and authority."

"We procrastinate because of fearing the outcome, failing to complete projects."

The false-self uses our mental energy and our emotional energy to compulsively run its ego program.

Patience is not the ability to wait, but the ability to keep a good attitude while waiting.

Exercise

What have I learned about how the false-self of Type Six keeps me in my ego trance?

ENNEAGRAM POINT SEVEN

Point Seven – The Joyful Guardian of Gratitude

The Holy Idea is Holy Plan, seeing that there is a specific design to evolution and transformation and we don't need to meddle with it; the Holy Work is letting ourselves trust and be in the present, doing what is appropriate and necessary right now. Openness to the joy of the unfolding reality of life. Open-ended wonder and curiosity.

When we are in Type Seven wholeness we are open and joyous. We are full of ideas, optimistic and spontaneous.

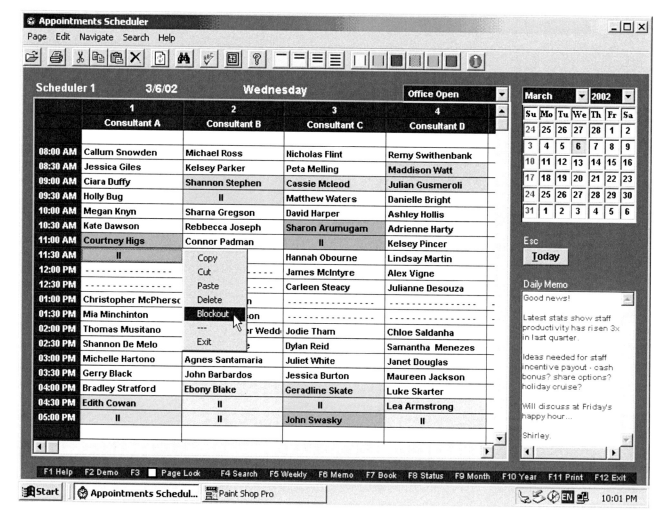

What Sevens tell us when their drinking/using "was working":

"I drank because it was fun."

"I drank to feel free."

"I liked to party and if I used I could party longer."

The false-self of the Type Seven tries to imitate the real essence quality: The ego creates fake freedom. The ego creates options thinking that options (fake freedom) will create happiness. But the ego does not want to choose, because in choosing that would limit the options and what the false-self believes is freedom. The external opportunity for freedom becomes a substitute for connecting with an internal sense of freedom.

Basic False-Self Proposition: Pain and frustration can be avoided and the good life assured by inventing options, opportunities, and adventures.

Habitual False-Self Focus of Attention: The positive in all things.

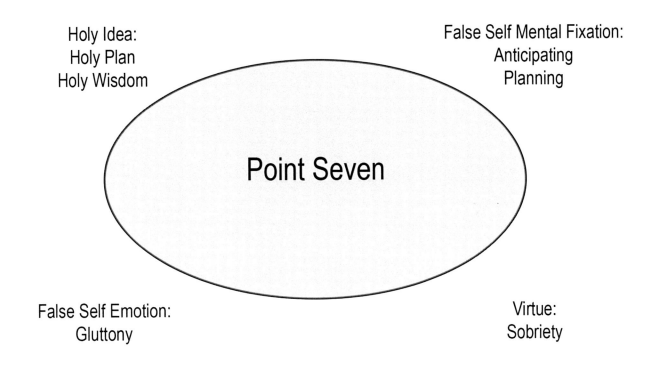

Holy Idea:
Holy Plan
Holy Wisdom

False Self Mental Fixation:
Anticipating
Planning

Point Seven

False Self Emotion:
Gluttony

Virtue:
Sobriety

Exercise for the Type Seven

When my drinking/using "was working" I drank/used because:

_____

_____

_____

_____

_____

_____

_____

_____

_____

_____

_____

_____

_____

_____

_____

_____

_____

_____

What Sevens tell us about themselves when they are in their false-self compulsion:

"Life is an adventure and I must continually plan for the adventure."

"We are pleasure-seeking and gluttons for experience and enjoyment."

"We must always be optimistic, active, and energetic."

"We see multiple options but have difficulty with commitment and do not want to put limits on ourselves."

"We are afraid of choosing one thing for fear of missing something else."

The false-self uses our mental energy and our emotional energy to compulsively run its ego program.

Exercise

What have I learned about how the false-self of Type Seven keeps me in my ego trance?

ENNEAGRAM POINT EIGHT

Point Eight – The Truth Protector

The Holy Idea is Holy Truth, which helps us understand what exists beneath the appearance of things. The real quality comes from being in the body, a sense of aliveness and immediacy to reality.

When we are in Type Eight wholeness we are decisive, present and powerful. We are big-hearted, strong, protective and determined, and not afraid to show our innocence, meaning our openness to what is unfolding.

What Eights tell us when their drinking/using "was working":

"I drank to keep plowing ahead."

"I drank so I didn't have to feel."

"I drank because "why not?" I was in charge."

"I drank to shut out the world and its demands."

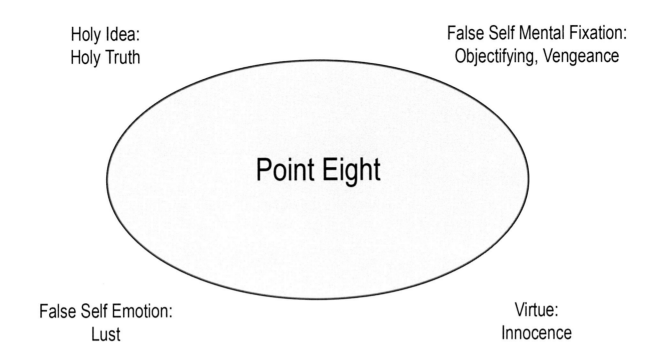

Holy Idea:
Holy Truth

False Self Mental Fixation:
Objectifying, Vengeance

Point Eight

False Self Emotion:
Lust

Virtue:
Innocence

<u>Exercise for the Type Eight</u>

When my drinking/using "was working" I drank/used because:

The false-self of the Type Eight tries to imitate the real essence quality: The ego wants this quality of realness and vitality, and it tries to recreate this by assertion; pushing to try to feel real. And, paradoxically the more intensely it asserts the more it is cut off from its heart and the less connected to the immediacy it wishes to feel.

Basic False-Self Proposition: Protection and respect are gained by becoming strong and powerful and by hiding vulnerability.

Habitual False-Self Focus of Attention: Power, Injustices and Control.

What Eights tell us about themselves when they are in their false-self compulsion:

"We want stimulation and excitement."

"We are concerned with strength and protecting the weak."

"We are direct, confrontational and express our anger immediately."

"We are aggressive, intimidating and impulsive."

"We deny our own vulnerability and weakness."

The false-self uses our mental energy and our emotional energy to compulsively run its ego program.

<u>Exercise</u>

What have I learned about how the false-self of Type Eight keeps me in my ego trance?

ENNEAGRAM POINT NINE

Type Nine – The Bringer of Acceptance and Equanimity

The Holy Idea is Holy Love, the heart of truth, the quality of lovableness of reality when it is seen without distortion, rather than through the filter of the ego. The real quality is a sense of dynamic energy of being at home. Openness to self, others and God.

When we are in Type Nine wholeness we are in a place of dynamic receptivity and oneness. We are calm and engaged but above all we have a sense of serenity in the activities of life.

What Nines tell us when their drinking/using "was working":

"I drank to be at peace."

"I drank so I didn't have to worry about the demands of everyone else."

"I drank because, as a minister, it made me feel more connected to God."

"I drank to avoid the conflict in my life."

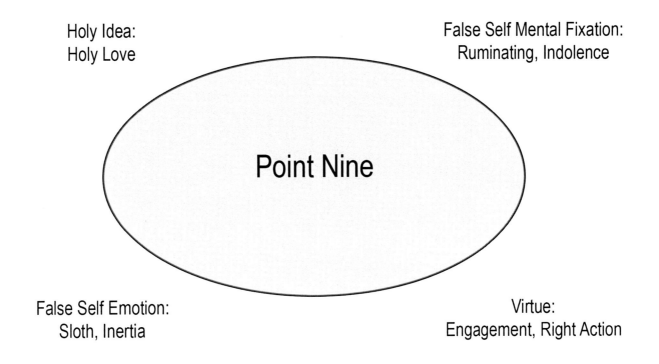

Holy Idea:
Holy Love

False Self Mental Fixation:
Ruminating, Indolence

Point Nine

False Self Emotion:
Sloth, Inertia

Virtue:
Engagement, Right Action

Exercise for the Type Nine

When my drinking/using "was working" I drank/used because:

_____

_____

_____

_____

_____

_____

_____

_____

_____

_____

_____

_____

_____

_____

_____

_____

_____

_____

_____

The false-self of the Type Nine tries to imitate the real essence quality: The ego tries to protect the sense of peace and oneness by not engaging. "Spirituality" is a favorite way for a nine to check out here. The nine retreats into an inner world to get the illusion of peace, rather than being dynamically present in the world in a centered peaceful way.

Basic False-Self Proposition: Belonging and comfort are gained by attending to and merging with others and by dispersing energy into non-essential activities and activities important to others.

Habitual False-Self Focus of Attention: The inessential and the agenda of others.

The biggest human temptation is to settle for too little.
-Thomas Merton

What Nines tell us about themselves when they are in their false-self compulsion:

"We see all sides to every issue as peacemakers and harmonizers."

"We avoid conflict and want the comfortable solution."

"We have difficulty saying 'no'."

"We are ambivalent about our own needs and wants."

"We 'go along to get along'."

"We self forget."

"We busy ourselves with the priorities of others, not our own."

The false-self uses our mental energy and our emotional energy to compulsively run its ego program.

<u>Exercise</u>

What have I learned about how the false-self of Type Nine keeps me in my ego trance?

How the Enneagram Applies to Me

Mediator - Peacemaker
Connector - Harmonizer

Boss - Leader
Challenger - Protector

Perfectionist - Reformer
Crusader - Moralist

Epicure - Generalist
Visionary - Connoiseur

Giver - Helper
Caretaker - Enabler

Devil's Advocate - Loyalist
Questioner - Skeptic

Performer - Achiever
Succeeder - Initiator

Observer - Recluse
Thinker - Investigator

Tragic - Romantic - Artist
Aesthete - Individualist

Exercise:

Recognizing Part of Each Type is in Me

Having reviewed all nine types, their essence and the way the false-self ego tries to get back to essence, and in so doing blocks our being in essence, what I notice about each type that resonates with me:

I relate to Type One- the PERFECTIONIST/REFORMER in the following ways:

_____

_____

_____

_____

_____

_____

_____

I relate to Type Two – the HELPER/GIVER in the following ways:

_____

_____

_____

_____

I relate to Type Three – the PERFORMER/ACHIEVER in the following ways:

I relate to Type Four – the ARTIST/INDIVIDUALIST in the following ways:

I relate to Type Five – the OBSERVER/INVESTIGATOR in the following ways:

I relate to Type Six – the LOYAL SKEPTIC/DEVIL'S ADVOCATE in the following ways:

I relate to Type Seven – the EPICURE/GENERALIST in the following ways:

I relate to Type Eight – the LEADER/CHALLENGER in the following ways:

I relate to Type Nine – the PEACEMAKER/MEDIATOR in the following ways:

The Impact of Addictions on Our Type

As mentioned in the Introduction, we all have a false-self, a persona and character defects that develop with our ego in childhood in order to navigate the world. While it is necessary for our development and survival in our families to construct this false-self (or ego), just like our addictions, it becomes a barrier to a full experience living a spiritual life.

Addictions intensify the false-self through denial, exaggerated character defects and instincts gone astray. As we said it "super-sizes" the false-self.

The Steps are a means to deconstruct the false-self. As we spend more time in recovery, we find that the false-self and our character defects are trickier and more subtle than we had expected. We may find it difficult to stay sober by using the Steps alone and/or we do not live lives that are as happy, joyous and free as we had hoped.

The Enneagram—because it speaks to the subtle differences in our personalities and motivations is a tool to deepened and supplement the Twelve Steps so we can find this joy and freedom and live a more spiritual life.

There will come a time when you believe everything is finished.

That will be the beginning.

- Louis L'Amour

False-Self Energies By Type

Signs that your false-self compulsion is energizing your thoughts, feelings and actions.

Type One   Notice harsh judgments, impatience, self-criticism.

Type Two   Notice when you're complaining, feeling unappreciated. How do you become depleted? What happens when you say 'no'?

Type Three   Pay attention to the feeling of "making it happen myself" as efficiently as possible, gaining recognition. How important is your image in other's eyes? What do you do to be admired, respected?

Type Four   Notice when you're comparing your self, your situation, your satisfaction to others. Be aware when you want what you believe others have and why you don't.

Type Five   Notice when pessimism comes up, feelings of isolation, concern about your resources of time and energy.

Type Six   Ask yourself, "What's the worst that could happen…and what would I really do?" Notice where the feeling of worry and anxiety are in your body. Where does your mind go?

Type Seven   Pay attention to feeling limited or trapped. Notice when you get anxious and impatient with unpleasant feelings. When do you overbook yourself?

Type Eight   Become aware of your desire to take control. Notice when things seem black and white – right or wrong – worth it or not. What happens when you start to feel vulnerable?

Type Nine   Ask yourself how you REALLY feel about something. Notice when you want to avoid conflict and withdraw. How often do you go along to get along?

What I notice about the False-Self Energy of My Type is:

_____

_____

_____

_____

_____

_____

_____

_____

_____

_____

_____

FALSE-SELF ENERGY IS OFTEN IN THE FORM OF AVOIDANCE OR RESISTANCE.
– WHAT EACH TYPE AVOIDS OR RESISTS –

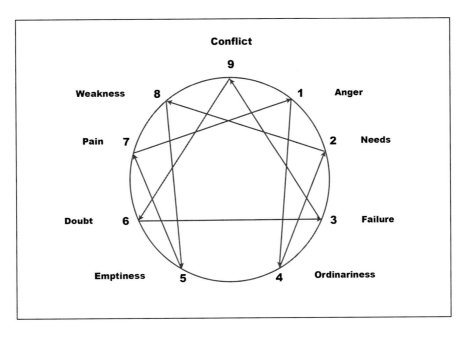

<u>Exercise</u>

How do I experience the energy of my false-self in my body, my thinking and my emotions?

Part III
TAKING THE STEPS WITH THE HELP OF THE ENNEAGRAM

Identifying your Type

I believe my type is a:

_____

The essence (highest state) of my type is:

_____

_____

_____

_____

_____

_____

_____

When I am in a place of serenity and respond to the world from my essence, I have the following characteristics:

_____

_____

When I am irritable, lonely or discontent or otherwise just out of touch with my essence spiritually, my false-self or character defects are going to act out compulsively to try to make me feel okay. When they do…

I have these kind of thoughts:

I have these kind of feelings:

I have these kind of instinctive compulsions to do:

STEP ONE

"We admitted we were powerless over alcohol—that our lives had become unmanageable."

The purpose of Step One is to experience a surrender to reality—an emotional recognition that our ego outlook is not how life is.

<u>Step One Barriers of Type</u>

Type One	the need to keep the perfect illusion going—what if others find out I am imperfect?
Type Two	the focus on others preventing connecting with self to surrender—how could someone so giving be an addict?
Type Three	the need for external approval preventing self surrender—isn't being successful proof that I am not an addict?
Type Four	the need to feel intensity of emotions prevents clarity of seeing powerlessness—will I lose my power to be unique?
Type Five	a resistance to feeling deeply allows a Five not to take Step One in an emotional way, a holding back from embracing powerlessness; a need to have more information—where is the proof?
Type Six	inability to trust prevents surrender—what am I supposed to believe in?
Type Seven	surrender implies options are limited, this is a barrier—will I have to give up having fun and doing what I want?
Type Eight	surrender implies do not have power—who else will be in charge?
Type Nine	surrender requires stepping more into life—how can I be comfortable?

> # There is a difference between giving up, and knowing when you have had enough.

Taking Step One by Type

Type One We surrender the need to keep the perfect illusion going. When we do we can admit that we are powerless over alcohol and that our lives have become unmanageable.

Type Two We surrender our focus on others in order to see ourselves clearly. When we see ourselves clearly we can admit that we are powerless over alcohol and that our lives have become unmanageable.

Type Three We surrender our need for external approval. When we do, we can honestly admit that we are powerless over alcohol and that our lives have become unmanageable.

Type Four We surrender our need to engage our emotions which block us from clearly seeing. When we see clearly we can now admit that we are powerless over alcohol and that our lives have become unmanageable.

Type Five We surrender our need to have more information and when we do we can admit that we are powerless over alcohol and that our lives have become unmanageable.

Type Six We surrender our fear and anxiety about surrendering. When we do we can admit that we are powerless over alcohol and that our lives have become unmanageable.

Type Seven We surrender our need to always have another option. When we do we can honestly admit that we are powerless over alcohol and that our lives have become unmanageable.

Type Eight We surrender our need to have power and control. When we do we can honestly admit that we are powerless over alcohol and that our lives have become unmanageable.

Type Nine We surrender our need to stay disengaged from our lives. When we do we can admit that we are powerless over alcohol and that our lives have become unmanageable.

> **When you have to start compromising yourself or your morals for the people around you, it's probably time to change the people around you.**

In Step One we admit that when we are in our compulsion we are powerless. We think the thoughts our false-self wants us to think. We have the feelings our false-self wants us to have and we instinctively act the way our false-self wants us to act. When this happens our life is truly unmanageable.

In taking Step One again right now I, _____, surrender to the fact that this compulsive false-self has continually controlled my life. In my surrender I begin the process of developing awareness of when my false-self is running my life.

The Steps are meant to be taken by all three Enneagram domains, that is by the mind, the emotions and the bodily experience.

For people of my type, _____, some of the biggest barriers to taking the first step in this three-fold way are:

_____

_____

_____

_____

_____

_____

_____

_____

_____

_____

_____

_____

_____

_____

_____

_____

_____

Taking Step One by My Type

I surrender:

And when I do I can admit that I am powerless over alcohol and that my life has become unmanageable.

STEP TWO

"We came to believe that a power greater than ourselves could restore us to sanity."

The purpose of Step Two is to experience that there is something outside our ego which if we orient our lives toward it allows us to live sanely.

<u>Step Two Barriers of Type</u>

Type One   out of touch with the somatic qualities of belief, belief is hard because the mind goes all over the place.

Type Two   out of touch with self so its hard to surrender to God, if we have made a god out of others

Type Three   out of touch with inner approval, don't have an internalized connection to God to surrender to—lack of inner connection

Type Four	the internal emotional reality seems more real than an Other (God)
Type Five	logically the five can see this, but emotionally the five can be so out of touch that they can't believe/experience it
Type Six	does not trust sufficiently to believe
Type Seven	to believe this would cut off other options
Type Eight	the ego does not want to take a back seat to some greater power
Type Nine	the nine can believe it in an indifferent kind of way but not in a dynamic way that actually causes change.

The second step is a recognition that our own willfulness, our own ego, is the problem. We need help outside of ourselves if we are going to recover and live in our essence.

The Steps are meant to be taken by all three Enneagram domains, that is by the mind, the emotions and the bodily experience. For people of my type, _____, some of the biggest barriers to taking the second step in this three-fold way are:

_____

_____

_____

_____

_____

_____

_____

_____

Taking Step Two by My Type

I came to believe that if I became able to break the automatic patterns of my false-self compulsion by:

_____

_____

_____

_____

_____

_____

_____

_____

_____

_____

_____

...that a power greater than me would restore me to sanity.

STEP THREE

"We made a decision to turn our will and our lives over to the care of God as we understood him."

Step Three makes it clear that to make this shift in orientation requires that we must realize we have a false-self to shed; we cannot do this without believing that there is something we can orient to that can sustain us.

<u>Step Three Barriers of Type</u>

Type One   may be too judgmental about the idea of God to turn will/life over

Type Two   is to used to giving to get, does not know how to turn life over to care that is unconditionally available

Type Three   making this decision runs against the ego grain that I can succeed no matter what

Type Four   can't get past our hopes it will just get better in the future to make this decision in the present

Type Five   is too out of touch with emotional values to make this kind of emotional decision

Type Six   does not trust HP

Type Seven   doesn't want to foreclose options, will experience loss by making this decision

Type Eight   not willing to lose power

Type Nine   too indecisive to make the decision

The Steps are meant to be taken by all three Enneagram domains, that is by the mind, the emotions and the bodily experience. For people of my type, _____, some of the biggest barriers to taking the third step in this three fold way are:

_____

_____

_____

Taking Step Three by My Type

I, _____, am becoming more fully aware that my ego, my false-self, my character defects are the guards to the prison I stay in when I am not in my essence. In Step Three I am making a decision to let God, as I understand him, open the door to that prison so I can be free.

I, _____, make the decision again right now to turn my thoughts and my feelings and my instinctive compulsion, that is my will and my life, over to the care of God as I understand Him.

I surrender my: _____

_____And in doing so it opens up a space outside my false-self from which I can decide right now. which I do, to turn my will and my life over to a power greater than me.

STEP FOUR

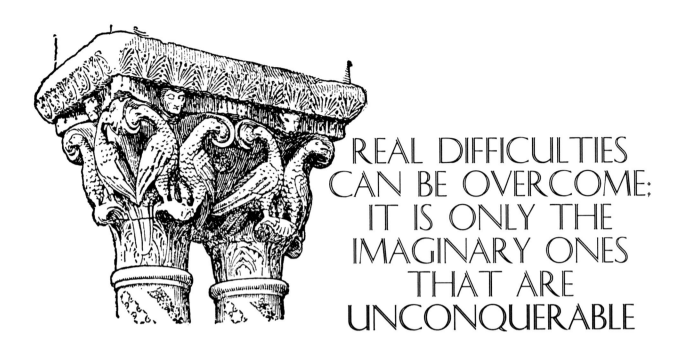

REAL DIFFICULTIES CAN BE OVERCOME; IT IS ONLY THE IMAGINARY ONES THAT ARE UNCONQUERABLE

"We made a searching and fearless moral inventory of ourselves."

The purpose of Step Four is to get a new attitude, a new relationship with our Creator to discover the obstacles in our path. (p.72, The *Big Book*)

To avoid falling into confusion over the names these defects should be called, let's take a universally recognized list of major human failings—the Seven Deadly Sins of pride, greed, lust, anger, gluttony, envy and sloth." (p.48, The *Twelve and Twelve*)

A Fourth Step is my inventory of the way that my false-self, my thoughts, my feelings, and my instinctive acting out, run my life.

> **"Life's challenges are not supposed to paralyze you, they're supposed to help you discover who you are."**
> **- Bernice Johnson Reagon**

Please turn to the Appendix to find the 4th Step inventory forms for your type.

The Steps are meant to be taken by all three Enneagram domains, that is by the mind, the emotions and the bodily experience. For people of my type, _____, some of the biggest barriers to taking the fourth step in this three fold way are:

STEP FIVE

"We admitted to God, to ourselves and to another human being the exact nature of our wrongs."

DON'T COMPARE
YOURSELF TO OTHERS.
COMPARE YOURSELF TO
THE PERSON FROM
YESTERDAY.

The only way that our awareness (the depth of our surrender) can help us see how our false-self has unconsciously driven our life is for us to admit to ourselves, and to another human being, and to God the exact nature of how this has occurred.

Step 5 is the essential to avoiding the Three Rs.

I first heard the Three Rs, not in a 12 Step setting, but in an Enneagram workshop:

> First they Run Us
> then they Rule Us
> then they Ruin Us

The Three Rs

First they Run Us
then they Rule Us
then they Ruin Us

The "they" the speaker was talking about was not our addiction to alcohol or other drugs, but the operation of the patterns of our false-self. Who would have thought that there could be something just as powerful as substance addiction unconsciously taking away our lives. Well, of course--the unconscious energy of our Enneagram type's false-self is what the illness inflates and what our knowledge of the Enneagram helps unlock for our path to joy, freedom and a new happiness.

The Steps are meant to be taken by all three Enneagram domains, that is by the mind, the emotions and the bodily experience. For people of my type, _____, some of the biggest barriers to taking the Fifth Step in this deep three-fold way are:

_____

_____

_____

_____

_____

_____

_____

_____

_____

_____

_____

_____

_____

_____

_____

_____

_____

_____

_____

_____

_____

_____

**It's not denial
I'm just very selective about the reality I accept**

STEP SIX

"We were entirely read to have God remove all these defects of character."

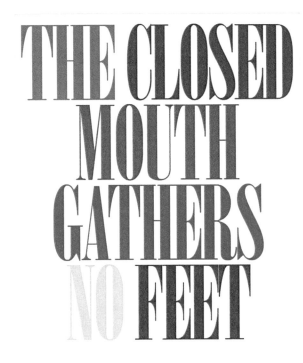

Once we develop some knowledge of the Enneagram, ego-driven false-self will come in and try to use that knowledge to continue to run the show. We will have some awareness, but we will be stuck. Step Six requires us to let our awareness continue to deepen our surrender, so that our patterns of compulsion can be removed by God. All challenges provide us with an opportunity to make a choice between our false-self compulsions and a deeper connection to our essence. Our false-self will use our Enneagram and recovery knowledge as a barrier to our moment to moment surrender. Having very helpful knowledge can be a way we can stay stuck trying to control rather than surrendering.

Steps Six and Seven Barriers by Type

Type One   the need to control the process

Type Two   the inability to be humble enough to let go to the process

Type Three   being out of touch with inner self, from which permission to let go comes

Type Four   inability to let go of the internal drama, if let go of control of process there is no drama

Type Five   the fact that the five cannot understand factually how it works, that is, how does HP remove character defects

Type Six   inability to trust prevents surrender to the process

Type Seven   surrender implies options are limited, this is a barrier

Type Eight   inability to feel helplessness

Type Nine   surrender to the process requires stepping more vigorously into life, to not really step in is faux surrender

The Steps are meant to be taken by all three Enneagram domains, that is by the mind, the emotions and the bodily experience. For people of my type, _____, some of the biggest barriers to taking the Sixth Step in this deep three-fold way are:

STEP SEVEN

"We humbly asked Him to remove our shortcomings."

Step Seven is another recognition that our ego-driven false-self is constantly trying to control our recovery. We will also see that even when our false-self tries to control something good, like our recovery, by its very nature it will block us from being in our essence and being spiritually connected with God. We must allow the awareness of the extent of our false-self wanting to run the show to deepen our surrender, to give us real humility, not to let our Enneagram and recovery knowledge feed our false-self's ego need to control.

I AM
NOT WHAT I HAVE
DONE,
I AM WHAT I
HAVE SURRENDERED

The Steps are meant to be taken by all three Enneagram domains, that is by the mind, the emotions and the bodily experience. For people of my type, _____, some of the biggest barriers to taking the Seventh Step in this deep three-fold way are:

_____

_____

_____

_____

_____

_____

_____

_____

_____

_____

_____

_____

_____

_____

_____

_____

_____

_____

_____

_____

STEP EIGHT

"We made a list of all persons we had harmed, and became willing to make amends to them all."

Step Eight is about building active awareness to be able to take action to free our essences of the power of the mistakes of the false-self. It is having an awareness of the wreckage and preparing to make amends to ameliorate the damage we have caused so that the compulsion of the false-self subsides. Becoming willing is about not letting our false-self (which seeks to protect us from the consequences of our actions) control our behavior any longer.

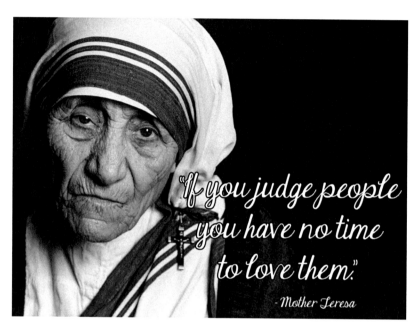

The Steps are meant to be taken by all three Enneagram domains, that is by the mind, the emotions and the bodily experience. For people of my type, _____, some of the biggest barriers to taking the Eighth Step in this deep three-fold way are:

_____

_____

_____

_____

_____

_____

_____

_____

_____

_____

_____

STEP NINE

"An eye for an eye will make the whole world blind"

-Gandhi

"We made direct amends to such people wherever possible, except when to do so would injure them or others."

Step Nine is about experiencing the awareness of how we caused harm. We then take the action to free our essence from the power of the mistakes of the false-self and make amends for our mistakes to lessen the injury we have caused. Our false-self is our psychic protection. As long as we have outstanding harms to others that are not amended, our psyche is going to channel energy into our false-self to make us feel protected from what we have done. We remain emotionally, energetically and spiritually not free.

The Steps are meant to be taken by all three Enneagram domains, that is by the mind, the emotions and the bodily experience. For people of my type, _____, some of the biggest barriers to taking the Ninth Step in this deep three-fold way are:

_____

_____

_____

_____

_____

_____

_____

_____

_____

_____

_____

Barriers by Type to Making Cleansing Step Nine Amends

One   the need to do it perfectly and the fear of being judged

Two   the lack of humility needed to make amends

Three   the need for approval about performing/making amends right

Four   the difficulty is being in the present and not getting caught up in what calamities the amends might precipitate

Five   the ability to hold back in an emotional way and not whole-heartedly make amends because of fear of emotional overwhelm

Six   inability to trust the process, worrying about what will be the outcome of making the amends

Seven   the feeling that making amends will cut off options with others and ourselves

Eight   the failure to emotionally experience the amends and fear of not having control of the process

Nine   desire to avoid conflict

Exercise

What are my barriers to making deep, cleansing amends?

STEP TEN

Whatever you think
the world is withholding
from you, you are
withholding
from the world.

- Eckhart Tolle

Step Ten is about continually building awareness to deepen our humility. We must be aware that our greater Enneagram knowledge can allow our recovery ego to grow. Our Enneagram knowledge received as spiritual guidance leads us to be more compassionate and humble, not more of a recovery authority.

Page 86 of the *Big Book* tells us how to take this inventory, and if we apply an Enneagram template, it tells us that by type.

Type One	Were we resentful?
Type Five	Were we selfish?
Type Three	Were we dishonest?
Type Six	Were we afraid?
Type Eight	Owe an apology?
Type Seven	Have we kept something to ourselves that should be discussed with another person at once?
Type Two	Were we kind and loving toward all?
All Types	What could we have done better?
Type Four	Were we thinking of ourselves most of the time?
Type Nine	Were we thinking of what we could pack into the stream of life?

This is what the Enneagram of Step Ten looks like.

Enneagram of Step Ten

Were we thinking of what we could
pack into the stream of life?

9

Owe an apology? **8**

1 Were we resentful?

Have we kept something to **7**
ourselves that should be
discussed with another
person at once?

2 Were we kind and loving
toward all?

Were we afraid? **6**

3 Were we dishonest?

Were we selfish? **5**

4 Were we thinking of ourselves most
of the time?

What insights does the Enneagram of Step Ten suggest to you?

If we connect the Enneagram of Step Ten with the Holy ideas, or the ideas of wholeness that are the fruit of working a daily Step Ten, then these are the gifts we get.

Big Book p.86 Question	Applies to:	Holy Idea	Gift
Were we resentful?	Type One	Holy Perfection	Serenity
Were we selfish?	Type Five	Holy Omniscience	Non-attachment
Were we dishonest?	Type Three	Holy Hope	Honesty
Were we afraid?	Type Six	Holy Faith	Courage
Owe an apology?	Type Eight	Holy Truth	Innocence
Have we kept some-thing to ourselves that should be dis-cussed with another person at once?	Type Seven	Holy Plan	Sobriety
Were we kind and loving toward all?	Type Two	Holy Will	Humility
What could we have done better?	All Types		
Were we thinking of ourselves most of the time?	Type Four	Holy Origin	Equanimity
Were we thinking of what we could pack into the stream of life?	Type Nine	Holy Love	Right Action

The Steps are meant to be taken by all three Enneagram domains, that is by the mind, the emotions and the bodily experience. For people of my type, _____, some of the biggest barriers to taking the Tenth Step in this deep three-fold way are:

To get the most benefit out of our Enneagram knowledge in doing Step Ten. In addition to taking Step Ten on a daily basis in the manner set out on page 86 of the *Big Book* it is helpful to add from a Step Ten Enneagram inventory four to six additional Enneagram inquiries related just to our Type. This will assure that our awareness of our false-self continues to grow and that we are more able to act from our three-entered essence.

Enneagram Accountability
Type One

Indicate a percentage for the time of during the day the trait or quality was present:

- Fully present in my body
- Connected to and holding center
- Meeting fear directly from center
- Listening at a deep level and staying curious
- Making decisions by listening fully to heart, head, instinctual center and God
- Choosing not to feel imperfect
- Reaching out and taking action to be a part of and belong to the wholeness of life
- Taking action to show my emotional truth
- Staying with and not running from my anger
- Moving toward an uncomfortable emotion
- Holding an uncomfortable emotion in awareness and awareness of breath at the same time
- Being 100% into my life
- Was I able to stay with longing without needing to escape it?
- Was I connected to others without being judgmental?
- Was I able to be aware of the way I constantly evaluate what is good and bad?
- Was I able to appreciate that there is more than one "right" way to do something and that other wrong ways may simply be individual differences?
- Was I able to accept that I am perfect in my own imperfection and that others are perfect in their own imperfections?
- Did I engage in physical activities in which I could be embodied?
- Did I use my awareness of my resentments as a clue to my suppressed wants or desires?
- Did I avoid getting caught in the illusion that I must be good/right in order to be worthy and loved?
- Did I allow myself free time for pleasure, relaxation and play?
- Did I find refuge from my inner critic in God's love for me?
- Was I connected to God?
- Was I aware of the physical sensations of being connected to God and being in God's presence?
- Was I able to do something special today to celebrate being alive?

Enneagram Accountability
Type Two

Indicate a percentage for the time of during the day the trait or quality was present:

- Fully present to my needs
- Connected to and holding center
- Listening at a deep level and staying curious
- Making decisions by listening fully to heart, head, instinctual center and God
- Feel appreciated and cared for by others
- Taking action to show my emotional truth
- Staying with and not running from my anger
- Moving toward an uncomfortable emotion
- Holding an uncomfortable emotion in awareness and awareness of breath at the same time
- Being 100% into my life
- Was I able to stay with longing without needing to escape it?
- Was I connected to others without being dependent on others?
- Was I able to realize that being loved does not depend upon changing myself or others?
- Was I able to gain clarity about who the real me is and about my own wants and needs?
- Was I able to realize that my anger is a signal of my own neediness, and was I able to except my own neediness?
- Was I able to accept that I am not indispensable?
- Was I able to allow myself to give and to receive without expectation?
- Was I able to have appropriate boundaries in my life?
- Was I aware when my attempts to be helpful were intrusive or controlling?
- Was I aware when I was attempting to play God in somebody else's life?
- Was I connected to God?
- Was I aware of the physical sensations of being connected to God and being in God's presence?
- Was I able to do something special today to celebrate being alive?

Enneagram Accountability
Type Three

Indicate a percentage for the time of during the day the trait or quality was present:

- Fully present and connected to my inner knowing
- Connected to and holding center
- Listening at a deep level and staying curious
- Making decisions by listening fully to heart, head, instinctual center and God
- Taking action to show my emotional truth
- Staying with and not running from an uncomfortable emotion
- Moving toward an uncomfortable emotion
- Holding an uncomfortable emotion in awareness and awareness of breath at the same time
- Being 100% into my life
- Was I able to stay with longing without needing to escape it?
- Was I connected to others without being dependent on others?
- Was I aware that I am a worthy child of God and not dependent on approval from anyone else?
- Was I aware that my tendency to be over industrious and fast-paced is a way that I avoid connection with self?
- Did I welcome my emotions today?
- Did I stay connected with the values in my life that really matter?
- Did I practice looking inward for my own identity, separate and apart from what I do in the world?
- Did I set appropriate limits on my work?
- Did I practice patience?
- Did I practice empathy and understanding of others and self?
- Did I keep in awareness the realization that love comes from being, not from doing and having?
- Was I open to the experience of God's presence and aware that this presence was all I needed in order to feel okay?
- Was I connected to God?
- Was I aware of the physical sensations of being connected to God and being in God's presence?
- Was I able to do something special today to celebrate being alive?

Enneagram Accountability
Type Four

Indicate a percentage for the time of during the day the trait or quality was present:

- Fully present to the external world
- Connected to what is valuable to me and not adrift in my own feelings
- Meeting fear directly from center
- Listening at a deep level and staying curious
- Making decisions by listening fully to heart, head, instinctual center and God
- Choosing not to feel different but a part of
- Reaching out and taking action to be a part of and belong
- Taking action to show my emotional truth without having to dwell on it
- Holding an uncomfortable emotion in awareness and awareness of breath at the same time
- Being 100% into my life
- Was I able to stay with longing without making it a big emotional deal?
- Was I connected to others without being dependent on others?
- Was I able to focus on what is positive in my life rather than on what appears to be missing?
- Was I able to maintain a consistent course of action despite fluctuating feelings?
- Did I realize that I am not my feelings?
- Was I able to respond from a centered place rather than from an intense emotional reaction?
- Was I able to experience the beauty of ordinary life?
- Was I able to appreciate the realization that whenever I am caught in feelings of my own uniqueness I cut myself off from the experience of life?
- Was I able to take consistent actions based on my values without getting bogged down by my changing moods or fluctuating emotions?
- Did I realize that I can always meet God in the present in any moment?
- Was I aware that being at peace and calm and centered in God is a much deeper experience than being in an intense emotional experience?
- Was I aware that God is found in the ordinariness of life, not in a romantic ideal?
- Was I aware that when I feel different from others I am cutting myself off from God's presence?
- Was I connected to God?
- Was I aware of the physical sensations of being connected to God and being in God's presence?
- Was I able to do something special today to celebrate being alive?

Enneagram Accountability
Type Five

Indicate a percentage for the time of during the day the trait or quality was present:

- Fully present
- Connected to and holding center
- Meeting fear directly from center
- Listening to my feelings at a deep level and staying curious
- Making decisions by listening fully to heart, head, instinctual center and God
- Choosing not to feel rejected but a part of
- Reaching out and taking action to be a part of and belong
- Taking action to show my emotional truth
- Staying with and not running from an uncomfortable emotion
- Moving toward an uncomfortable emotion
- Holding an uncomfortable emotion in awareness and awareness of breath at the same time
- Being 100% into my life as a participant and not just an observer
- Was I able to stay with longing without needing to escape it by trying to understand it?
- Was I connected to others without being only an observer of others?
- Did I allow myself to fully experience my feelings instead of detaching and retreating into my mind?
- Was I aware of a pattern of withdrawal and did I recognize that my withdrawal and contraction invites intrusion?
- Was I aware that I have ample abundance in my life for everything I need to do?
- Was I able to live in the mystery of God's love for me in this life without needing to know or understand?
- Was I able to express gratitude today for the rich abundance in my life?
- Did I experience that when I am connected with God's presence I always have abundant energy for whatever I need to do in my life?
- Was I able to experience that my perspective on life is always partial?
- Was I connected to God?
- Was I aware of the physical sensations of being connected to God and being in God's presence?
- Was I able to do something special today to celebrate being alive?

Enneagram Accountability
Type Six

Indicate a percentage for the time of during the day the trait or quality was present:

- Fully present
- Connected to and holding center
- Meeting fear directly from center
- Listening at a deep level and staying curious
- Making decisions by listening fully to heart, head, instinctual center and God
- Forgiving those who have harmed me
- Forgiving those who intrude into my emotional space
- Choosing not to feel rejected but a part of
- Reaching out and taking action to be a part of and belong
- Taking action to show my emotional truth
- Staying with and not running from an uncomfortable emotion
- Moving toward an uncomfortable emotion
- Holding an uncomfortable emotion in awareness and awareness of breath at the same time
- Being 100% into my life
- Was I able to stay with longing without needing to escape it?
- Was I connected to others without being dependent on others?
- Did I act out of my own authority connected with God?
- Did I accept uncertainty in life as a part of God's mystery?
- Did I get caught up in busyness as a way to avoid experiencing anxiety?
- Did I live life with courage based on an awareness of God's love for me?
- Was I connected to God?
- Was I aware of the physical sensations of being connected to God and being in God's presence?
- Was I able to do something special today to celebrate being alive?

Enneagram Accountability
Type Seven

Indicate a percentage for the time of during the day the trait or quality was present:

- Fully present to my inner world
- Connected to and holding center
- Meeting fear directly from center
- Listening at a deep level and staying curious
- Making decisions by listening fully to heart, head, instinctual center and God
- Able to avoid temptations of excess
- Taking action to show my emotional truth
- Staying with and not running from an uncomfortable emotion
- Moving toward an uncomfortable emotion
- Holding an uncomfortable emotion in awareness and awareness of breath at the same time
- Being 100% into my life
- Was I able to stay with longing without needing to escape it?
- Was I connected to others without being dependent on others?
- Did not notice when my quests for pleasure both options was part of an emotionally reactive pattern so I could avoid experiencing a difficult emotion to?
- Did I experience freedom in commitment?
- Was I able to focus on one thing at a time which best allows me to do my work and stay connected to the presence of God?
- Was I able to stay 100% in the present?
- Was I aware when I used planning for the future as a way to avoid being present?
- Was I able to make and keep commitments to myself and others and God?
- Was I able to slow down my activities so I could feel compassion for others and myself?
- Am I aware of when I make the same mistake over and over because of my desire to avoid experiencing the pain of that mistake the first time?
- Am I aware of when I'll avoid experiencing uncomfortable emotions by feeling entitled and superior?
- Was I connected to God?
- Was I aware of the physical sensations of being connected to God and being in God's presence?
- Was I able to do something special today to celebrate being alive?

Enneagram Accountability
Type Eight

Indicate a percentage for the time of during the day the trait or quality was present:

- Fully present to my inner feelings
- Connected to and holding center
- Listening at a deep level and staying curious
- Making decisions by listening fully to heart, head, instinctual center and God
- Taking action to show my emotional truth
- Staying with and not running from an uncomfortable emotion
- Moving toward an uncomfortable emotion
- Holding an uncomfortable emotion in awareness and awareness of breath at the same time
- Being 100% into my life
- Was I able to stay with longing without needing to escape it?
- Was I connected to others without being dependent on others?
- Was I aware that my own strong and powerful assertion is a defense to my vulnerability?
- Was I able to be dependent upon other people for things I need?
- Was I able to practice being vulnerable and open to tender feelings?
- Was I able to practice waiting and listening before taking action as a way to moderate my impulsivity?
- Was I able to stay connected to my calm inner being, and my connection with God that comes from being connected to my inner being?
- Was I aware that my truth is always a limited perspective?
- Was I able to seek win-win solutions with others?
- Was I able to compromise and increase my connection with self and others?
- Was not able to understand that my view of what is fair is always a limited perspective?
- Was I able to wake up and maintain awareness instead of falling asleep in control patterns, or excessive materialism or low-level comfort?
- Was I connected to God?
- Was I aware of the physical sensations of being connected to God and being in God's presence?
- Was I able to do something special today to celebrate being alive?

Enneagram Accountability
Type Nine

Indicate a percentage for the time of during the day the trait or quality was present:

- Fully present to my life
- Connected to and holding center
- Meeting fear directly from center
- Listening at a deep level and staying curious
- Making decisions by listening fully to heart, head, instinctual center and God
- Take a position for what is important to me
- Choosing not to feel rejected but a part of
- Taking action to show my emotional truth
- Staying with and not running from an uncomfortable emotion
- Moving toward an uncomfortable emotion
- Holding an uncomfortable emotion in awareness and awareness of breath at the same time
- Being 100% into my life
- Was I able to stay with longing without needing to escape it?
- Was I connected to others without being dependent on others?
- Was I able to realize that blending in and the comfort of belonging are not substitutes for love and work?
- Was I able to pay attention to my own spiritual needs and physical well-being?
- Was I able to be aware that my own anger and frustration is a signal that I am neglecting something inside me that matters?
- Was I able to avoid the trance of TV, food, errands or chores blocking me from accessing my real priorities?
- Was I able to avoid ruminating and being stuck in ruminating, in order to avoid taking action?
- Was I able to accept discomfort and change as a natural part of life?
- Was I able to accept that God is in the chaos as much as the order?
- Was I able to stay in God's presence in times of change, uncertainty and ambiguity?
- Was I connected to God?
- Was I aware of the physical sensations of being connected to God and being in God's presence?
- Was I able to do something special today to celebrate being alive?

STEP ELEVEN

"Sought through prayer and meditation to improve our conscious contact with God as we understood Him, praying only for knowledge of his will for us and the power to carry that out."

Step Eleven is about using contemplative practices to calm the compulsion of the false-self. It is a proactive program, which when undertaken will undermine the energy of the false-self.

The Steps are meant to be taken by all three Enneagram domains, that is by the mind, the emotions and the bodily experience. For people of my type, _____, some of the biggest barriers to taking the Eleventh Step in this deep three-fold way are:

Together the Enneagram and the Steps tell us what we need to break through the prickly barriers of our false-self constructs.

PLEASE CUT ALONG THE LINE AND TAKE WHAT YOU NEED

KINDNESS

HOPE

CHANGE

TIME

PATIENCE

LOVE

STRENGTH

PEACE

We are best able to discern God's will when we are present.

Enneagram Invocation

I now remember that I am here and present in the moment.
I am grounded, alive, and connected in my body.
I am open and receptive to the truth and compassion of my heart.
I am clear and awake to the stillness of Mind.
I bear witness to the Presence of God.

We are best able to discern God's will when we see God's essence in others.

Enneagram Greeting or Farewell

_____ I see the spark of your divine essence in you. Thank you, thank you, thank you for bringing your special divine essence into the world.

Sometimes a short Enneagram prayer can be very helpful to keep us conscious.

Prayer Mantras

Type One
> Thank you God for creating perfection every minute.

Type Two
> God, thank you for taking care of everyone.

Type Three
> God, hold me in stillness so I can more deeply experience your love and be your glory.

Type Four
> God, thank you for calling me to take action in my unique dance of beauty for your glory in this world.

Type Five
> God, in this moment let your abundance call me to open my heart and reach out in love.

Type Six
> God, thank you for holding me safe right now in the hands of your love.

Type Seven
> God, in the integrity of my commitment to you there is unbounded freedom.

Type Eight
> God, in the protection of your ever present awesome power I love openly.

Type Nine
> God, thank you for allowing me to take action right now to be a part of your Joy.

STEP TWELVE

"Having had a spiritual awakening as the result of these Steps, we tried to carry this message to others and to practice these principles in our affairs."

Step Twelve is about broadening the surrender of our false-self to all areas of our lives, by taking action to be an example to others of a person living free in essence, and by allowing our surrender of our false-self to continue to unfold.

AFTER ALL OF THIS IS OVER, ALL THAT WILL HAVE REALLY MATTERED IS HOW WE TREATED EACH OTHER.

The Steps are meant to be taken by all three Enneagram domains, that is by the mind, the emotions and the bodily experience. For people of my type, _____, some of the biggest barriers to taking the Twelfth Step in this deep three-fold way are:

_____

_____

_____

_____

_____

_____

_____

_____

_____

_____

_____

_____

_____

_____

_____

_____

_____

i am thankful for absolutely everything.

As mentioned earlier our Enneagram Type tells us which of the Promises of recovery applies most specifically to us.

<u>The promises of the spiritual awakening of recovery for your type</u>

Type Seven	We are going to know a new freedom and a new happiness
Type Four	We will not regret the past nor wish to shut the door on it.
Type Nine	We will comprehend the word serenity and we will know peace.
Type Two	No matter how far down the scale we have gone, we will see how our experience can benefit others.
Type One	That feeling of uselessness and self pity will disappear.
Type Five	We will lose interest in selfish things and gain interest in our fellows.
Type Three	Self-seeking will slip away.
ALL Types	Our whole attitude and outlook upon life will change.
Type Six	Fear of people and of economic insecurity will leave us.
ALL Types	We will intuitively know how to handle situations which used to baffle us.
Type Eight	We will suddenly realize that God is doing for us what we could not do for ourselves.

-        Promises of AA, the _Big Book_

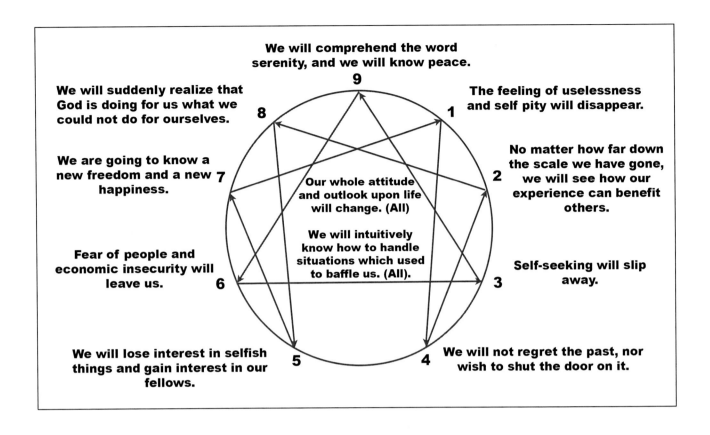

We will comprehend the word serenity, and we will know peace.

We will suddenly realize that God is doing for us what we could not do for ourselves.

The feeling of uselessness and self pity will disappear.

We are going to know a new freedom and a new happiness.

No matter how far down the scale we have gone, we will see how our experience can benefit others.

Our whole attitude and outlook upon life will change. (All)

We will intuitively know how to handle situations which used to baffle us. (All).

Fear of people and economic insecurity will leave us.

Self-seeking will slip away.

We will lose interest in selfish things and gain interest in our fellows.

We will not regret the past, nor wish to shut the door on it.

NOTHING SAYS LOVE LIKE COMPLETE ACCEPTANCE

Sought Through Prayer and Meditation Through the Lord's Prayer

Type Nine	Our Father which art in heaven (unifying principal)
Type One	Hallowed be thy name (not perfection but thy name)
Type Two	Thy kingdom come (not my kingdom)
Type Three	Thy will be done (not my will)
Type Four	On earth as it is in heaven (make the kingdom here and now, not there and then)
Type Five	Give us this day our daily bread (only what is necessary, not everything)
Type Six	Forgive us our trespasses as we forgive those who trespass against us (a temporal sequence)
Type Seven	Lead us not into temptation (the gluttony of exciting experiences, including, but not limited to, food and alcohol)
Type Eight	Deliver us from evil (Eights unconsciously can have a sense of shame, which feels like evil – a real fallacy. Their prayer is to be delivered from the evil of that feeling of shame of not being enough as they are, as God's child.)
Type Nine	For thine is the kingdom, the power and the glory, forever and ever (I am not fused with the universe, merely part of it.)

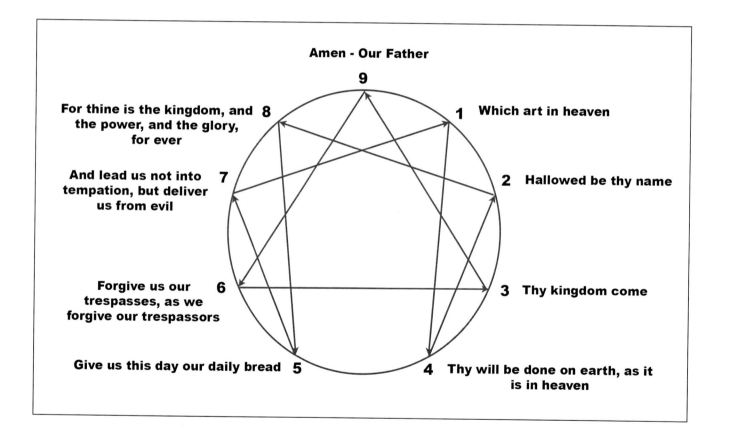

For Christians the Sermon on the Mount is one of the most powerful teachings in all of the Bible. In the Sermon on the Mount is an explicit direction for each Enneagram Type that allows the gifts of recovery to be practiced in all of our affairs.

Enneagram of the Sermon on the Mount

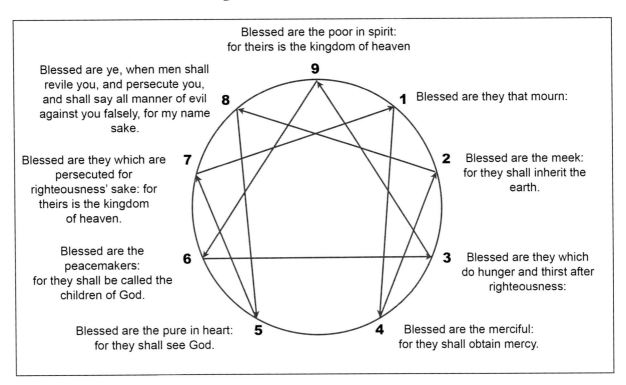

Sermon on the Mount Teachings and Blessings by Type

Type One
> For the One the blessing is to recognize honestly the conditions of life. The One's compulsive need for things to be perfect is the way to avoid accepting reality as it is. If we see reality clearly we do mourn. Judging and critiquing is a head process that keeps the one out of the heart center.

Type Two
> For the Two the blessing is humility. Humility allows for reliance on God and freedom from the pride of the false-self.

Type Three
> For the Three the blessing of thirsting after righteousness is to be emotionally right sized. The quality that allows one to become spiritually domesticated, where the ego self does not need to be out on parade.

Type Four
> For the Four the blessing is mercy. Mercy is a quality of emotion. Only with mercy is it possible to escape the Four's inner emotional turmoil.

Type Five
> For the Five the blessing is purity of heart. From the heart is the way we relate to others. Despite all our head knowledge, only through our relations with others is it possible to find our own authentic selves.

Type Six

For the Six the blessing is peace. The six longs to be a child of God free of worry and anxiety. By making peace with others the six is drawn into his own wholeness.

Type Seven

For the Seven the blessing is authenticity. It comes from taking a stand for what is right for the seven's authentic self. The kingdom of heaven is possible only when we give up all the other options. We can be self identified with money or power or fashion etc., but all of these are self referenced. All these options must be given up to become God referenced.

Type Eight

For the Eight the blessing is the right use power in the world for the sake of relationships, and not for the ego driven, power hungry false-self.

Type Nine

For the Nine the blessing is living in acknowledgement of one's dependence on God for wholeness. A dynamic interaction with God is needed. Love Blessing: Dynamic Connection to God.

Foot Work

Add Enneagram Recovery Tools to Your Toolkit

Get A Spiritual Director Who Uses The Enneagram.

Use Your Knowledge Of The Barriers For Your Type To Take The 12 Steps

Use Step Four Forms For Your Type

Take Daily Inventory Questions For Your Type

Use The Part Of The Lord's Prayer Related To Your Type To Focus On What Your Type Needs Spiritual Help On

Use A *CONNECT* Interactive Journal For Your Dominant Center (Mental, Emotional or Somatic) (Found At www.practicesofawakening.com)

Use Your Enneagram Prayer Mantra

Get Your Daily EnneaThought at www.enneagraminstitute.com

If You Are Christian Get a Free Christian Contemplative Daily Meditation Written By An Enneagram Author at www.cacradicalgrace.org

Practice Awareness Of The Energy Of Your Compulsion – the spot check inventory

Breathe Consciously to Create Space In The Energy Compulsion To Give Choice

APPENDIX
STEP 4

Review of Fears - ONE

INSTRUCTIONS FOR COMPLETION

1. In dealing with fears, we set them on paper. We listed people, institutions or principle with whom we were fearful (complete column 1 from top to bottom. Do nothing on columns 2, 3 or 4 until column 1 is complete).

2. We asked ourselves why do I have the fear (complete column 2 from top to bottom. Do nothing on columns 3 or 4 until column 2 is complete).

3. Which part of self caused the fear? Was it our self-esteem, our security, our ambitions, our personal or sex relations which had been interfered with? (complete each column within column 3 from top to bottom, starting with the self-esteem column and finishing with the sexual ambitions column. Do nothing on column 4 until column 3 is complete).

4. Referring to our list again, putting out of our minds the wrongs others have done, we resolutely looked for our own mistakes. Where had we been selfish, dishonest, self-seeking and frightened and inconsiderate? (asking ourselves the above questions, we complete column 4).

5. Reading from left to right, we now see the fear (column 1), why do I have the fear (column 2), the part of self that caused the fear (column 3) and the exact nature of the defect within us that allowed the fear to surface and block us from God's will (column 4).

Column 1 I'm fearful of:	Column 2 Why do I have the fear?	Self Column 3 AFFECTS MY (Which part of self caused the fear?)									Column 4 What is the exact nature of my wrongs, faults, mistakes, defects, shortcomings?							
		Social Instinct		Security Instinct		Sex Instinct		Ambitions			Selfish	Dishonest	Self-seeking & frightened	Inconsiderate	Being Judgmental	Being Resentful	Being Perfectionist	
		Self-Esteem	Personal relationships	Material	Emotional	Acceptable sex relations	Hidden Sex relations	Social	Security	Sexual								
1																		
2																		
3																		
4																		
5																		
6																		
7																		
8																		

Review of Resentments – ONE

INSTRUCTIONS FOR COMPLETION

1. In dealing with resentments, we set them on paper. We listed people, institutions or principles with whom we were angry (completely column 1 from top to bottom. Do nothing on columns 2, 3 or 4 until column 1 is complete).

2. We asked ourselves why we were angry (completely column 2 from top to bottom. Do nothing on columns 3 or 4 until column 2 is complete).

3. On our grudge list we set opposite each name our injuries. Was it our self-esteem, our security, our ambitions, our personal or sex relations which had been interfered with? (complete each column within column 3 from top to bottom, starting with the self-esteem column and finishing with the sexual ambitions column). Do nothing on column 4 until column 3 is complete).

4. Referring to our list again, putting out of our minds the wrongs others have done, we resolutely looked for our own mistakes. Where had we been selfish, dishonest, self-seeking and frightened and inconsiderate? (asking ourselves the above questions, we complete column 4).

5. Reading from left to right, we now see the resentment (column 1), the cause (column 2), the part of self that had been affected (column 3) and the exact nature of the defect within us that allowed the resentment to surface and block us from God's will (column 4).

	Column 1 I'm resentful at:	Column 2 The cause:	Self Column 3 AFFECTS MY (Which part of self is affected?)									Column 4 What is the exact nature of my wrongs, faults, mistakes, defects, shortcomings?							
			Social Instinct	Security Instinct		Sex Instinct		Ambitions										
			Self-Esteem	Personal relationships	Material	Emotional	Acceptable sex relations	Hidden Sex relations	Social	Security	Sexual	Selfish	Dishonest	Self-seeking & frightened	Inconsiderate	Being Judgmental	Being resentful	Being perfectionist
1																		
2																		
3																		
4																		
5																		
6																		
7																		
8																		

Review of our own sex conduct - ONE

INSTRUCTIONS FOR COMPLETION

1. We listed all the people we harmed (complete column 1 from top to bottom. Do nothing on columns 2, 3 or 4 until column 1 is complete).

2. We asked ourselves what we did (complete column 2 from top to bottom. Do nothing on columns 3 or 4 until column 2 is complete).

3. Was it our self-esteem, our security, our ambitions, our personal or sex relations that caused the harm? (complete each column within column 3 from top to bottom, starting with the self-esteem column and finishing with the sexual ambitions column. Do nothing on column 4 until column 3 is complete).

4. Referring to our list again, putting out of our minds the wrongs others had done, we resolutely looked for our own mistakes. Where had we been selfish, dishonest, self-seeking and frightened and inconsiderate? (asking ourselves the above questions, we complete column 4).

5. Reading from left to right, we now see the harm (column 1), what we did (column 2), the part of self that caused the harm (column 3) and the exact nature of the defect within us that caused the harm and blocked us from God's will (column 4).

	Column 1 Who did I harm?	Column 2 What did I do?	Self — Column 3 — AFFECTS MY (Which part of self caused the harm?)									Column 4 — What is the exact nature of my wrongs, faults, mistakes, defects, shortcomings?						
			Social Instinct		Security Instinct		Sex Instinct		Ambitions									
			Self-Esteem	Personal relationships	Material	Emotional	Acceptable sex relations	Hidden Sex relations	Social	Security	Sexual	Selfish	Dishonest	Self-seeking & frightened	Inconsiderate	Being Judgmental	Being resentful	Being perfectionist
1																		
2																		
3																		
4																		
5																		
6																		
7																		
8																		

Review of Fears - TWO

INSTRUCTIONS FOR COMPLETION

1. In dealing with fears, we set them on paper. We listed people, institutions or principle with whom we were fearful (complete column 1 from top to bottom. Do nothing on columns 2, 3 or 4 until column 1 is complete).

2. We asked ourselves why do I have the fear (complete column 2 from top to bottom. Do nothing on columns 3 or 4 until column 2 is complete).

3. Which part of self caused the fear? Was it our self-esteem, our security, our ambitions, our personal or sex relations which had been interfered with? (complete each column within column 3 from top to bottom, starting with the self-esteem column and finishing with the sexual ambitions column. Do nothing on column 4 until column 3 is complete).

4. Referring to our list again, putting out of our minds the wrongs others have done, we resolutely looked for our own mistakes. Where had we been selfish, dishonest, self-seeking and frightened and inconsiderate? (asking ourselves the above questions, we complete column 4).

5. Reading from left to right, we now see the fear (column 1), why do I have the fear (column 2), the part of self that caused the fear (column 3) and the exact nature of the defect within us that allowed the fear to surface and block us from God's will (column 4).

	Column 1 I'm fearful of:	Column 2 Why do I have the fear?	Self Column 3 AFFECTS MY (Which part of self caused the fear?)								Column 4 What is the exact nature of my wrongs, faults, mistakes, defects, shortcomings?							
			Social Instinct	Security Instinct		Sex Instinct		Ambitions			Selfish	Dishonest	Self-seeking & frightened	Inconsiderate	Being Possessive	Being Self-Important & having a false sense of humility	Trying to control others so they will like you
			Self-Esteem	Personal relationships	Material	Emotional	Acceptable sex relations	Hidden Sex relations	Social	Security	Sexual							
1																		
2																		
3																		
4																		
5																		
6																		
7																		
8																		

Review of Resentments – TWO

INSTRUCTIONS FOR COMPLETION

1. In dealing with resentments, we set them on paper. We listed people, institutions or principles with whom we were angry (completely column 1 from top to bottom. Do nothing on columns 2, 3 or 4 until column 1 is complete).

2. We asked ourselves why we were angry (completely column 2 from top to bottom. Do nothing on columns 3 or 4 until column 2 is complete).

3. On our grudge list we set opposite each name our injuries. Was it our self-esteem, our security, our ambitions, our personal or sex relations which had been interfered with? (complete each column within column 3 from top to bottom, starting with the self-esteem column and finishing with the sexual ambitions column). Do nothing on column 4 until column 3 is complete).

4. Referring to our list again, putting out of our minds the wrongs others have done, we resolutely looked for our own mistakes. Where had we been selfish, dishonest, self-seeking and frightened and inconsiderate? (asking ourselves the above questions, we complete column 4).

5. Reading from left to right, we now see the resentment (column 1), the cause (column 2), the part of self that had been affected (column 3) and the exact nature of the resentment to surface and block us from God's will (column 4).

Column 1 I'm resentful at:	Column 2 The cause:	Self — Column 3 AFFECTS MY (Which part of self is affected?)									Column 4 What is the exact nature of my wrongs, faults, mistakes, defects, shortcomings?						
		Social Instinct		Security Instinct		Sex Instinct		Ambitions									
		Self-Esteem	Personal relationships	Material	Emotional	Acceptable sex relations	Hidden Sex relations	Social	Security	Sexual	Selfish	Dishonest	Self-seeking & frightened	Inconsiderate	Being Possessive	Being Self-Important & having a false sense of humility	Trying to control others so they will like you
1																	
2																	
3																	
4																	
5																	
6																	
7																	
8																	

Review of our own sex conduct - TWO

INSTRUCTIONS FOR COMPLETION

1. We listed all the people we harmed (complete column 1 from top to bottom. Do nothing on columns 2, 3 or 4 until column 1 is complete).

2. We asked ourselves what we did (complete column 2 from top to bottom. Do nothing on columns 3 or 4 until column 2 is complete).

3. Was it our self-esteem, our security, our ambitions, our personal or sex relations that caused the harm? (complete each column within column 3 from top to bottom, starting with the self-esteem column and finishing with the sexual ambitions column. Do nothing on column 4 until column 3 is complete).

4. Referring to our list again, putting out of our minds the wrongs others had done, we resolutely looked for our own mistakes. Where had we been selfish, dishonest, self-seeking and frightened and inconsiderate? (asking ourselves the above questions, we complete column 4).

5. Reading from left to right, we now see the harm (column 1), what we did (column 2), the part of self that caused the harm (column 3) and the exact nature of the defect within us that caused the harm and blocked us from God's will (column 4).

	Column 1 Who did I harm?	Column 2 What did I do?	Self — Column 3 AFFECTS MY (Which part of self caused the harm?)										Column 4 What is the exact nature of my wrongs, faults, mistakes, defects, shortcomings?						
			Social Instinct		Security Instinct		Sex Instinct		Ambitions			Selfish	Dishonest	Self-seeking & frightened	Inconsiderate	Being Possessive	Being Self-Important & having a false sense of humility	Trying to control others so they will like you
			Self-Esteem	Personal relationships	Material	Emotional	Acceptable sex relations	Hidden Sex relations	Social	Security	Sexual							
1																		
2																		
3																		
4																		
5																		
6																		
7																		
8																		

Review of Fears - THREE

INSTRUCTIONS FOR COMPLETION

1. In dealing with fears, we set them on paper. We listed people, institutions or principle with whom we were fearful (complete column 1 from top to bottom. Do nothing on columns 2, 3 or 4 until column 1 is complete).

2. We asked ourselves why do I have the fear (complete column 2 from top to bottom. Do nothing on columns 3 or 4 until column 2 is complete).

3. Which part of self caused the fear? Was it our self-esteem, our security, our ambitions, our personal or sex relations which had been interfered with? (complete each column within column 3 from top to bottom, starting with the self-esteem column and finishing with the sexual ambitions column. Do nothing on column 4 until column 3 is complete).

4. Referring to our list again, putting out of our minds the wrongs others have done, we resolutely looked for our own mistakes. Where had we been selfish, dishonest, self-seeking and frightened and inconsiderate? (asking ourselves the above questions, we complete column 4).

5. Reading from left to right, we now see the fear (column 1), why do I have the fear (column 2), the part of self that caused the fear (column 3) and the exact nature of the defect within us that allowed the fear to surface and block us from God's will (column 4).

Column 1 I'm fearful of:	Column 2 Why do I have the fear?	Self Column 3 AFFECTS MY (Which part of self caused the fear?)									Column 4 What is the exact nature of my wrongs, faults, mistakes, defects, shortcomings?							
		Social Instinct		Security Instinct		Sex Instinct		Ambitions										
		Self-Esteem	Personal relationships	Material	Emotional	Acceptable sex relations	Hidden Sex relations	Social	Security	Sexual	Selfish	Dishonest	Self-seeking & frightened	Inconsiderate	Being vain and self promoting	Trying to look good	Being emotionally detached
1																	
2																	
3																	
4																	
5																	
6																	
7																	
8																	

INSTRUCTIONS FOR COMPLETION

1. In dealing with resentments, we set them on paper. We listed people, institutions or principles with whom we were angry (completely column 1 from top to bottom. Do nothing on columns 2, 3 or 4 until column 1 is complete).

2. We asked ourselves why we were angry (completely column 2 from top to bottom. Do nothing on columns 3 or 4 until column 2 is complete).

3. On our grudge list we set opposite each name our injuries. Was it our self-esteem, our security, our ambitions, our personal or sex relations which had been interfered with? (complete each column within column 3 from top to bottom, starting with the self-esteem column and finishing with the sexual ambitions column). Do nothing on column 4 until column 3 is complete).

4. Referring to our list again, putting out of our minds the wrongs others have done, we resolutely looked for our own mistakes. Where had we been selfish, dishonest, self-seeking and frightened and inconsiderate? (asking ourselves the above questions, we complete column 4).

5. Reading from left to right, we now see the resentment (column 1), the cause (column 2), the part of self that had been affected (column 3) and the exact nature of the defect within us that allowed the resentment to surface and block us from God's will (column 4).

Column 1 I'm resentful at:	Column 2 The cause:	Self Column 3 AFFECTS MY (Which part of self is affected?)									Column 4 What is the exact nature of my wrongs, faults, mistakes, defects, shortcomings?						
		Social Instinct		Security Instinct		Sex Instinct		Ambitions			Selfish	Dishonest	Self-seeking & frightened	Inconsiderate	Being vain and self-promoting	Trying to Look Good	Being emotionally detached
		Self-Esteem	Personal relationships	Material	Emotional	Acceptable sex relations	Hidden Sex relations	Social	Security	Sexual							
1																	
2																	
3																	
4																	
5																	
6																	
7																	
8																	

Review of our own sex conduct - THREE

INSTRUCTIONS FOR COMPLETION

1. We listed all the people we harmed (complete column 1 from top to bottom. Do nothing on columns 2, 3 or 4 until column 1 is complete).

2. We asked ourselves what we did (complete column 2 from top to bottom. Do nothing on columns 3 or 4 until column 2 is complete).

3. Was it our self-esteem, our security, our ambitions, our personal or sex relations that caused the harm? (complete each column within column 3 from top to bottom, starting with the self-esteem column and finishing with the sexual ambitions column. Do nothing on column 4 until column 3 is complete).

4. Referring to our list again, putting out of our minds the wrongs others had done, we resolutely looked for our own mistakes. Where had we been selfish, dishonest, self-seeking and frightened and inconsiderate? (asking ourselves the above questions, we complete column 4).

5. Reading from left to right, we now see the harm (column 1), what we did (column 2), the part of self that caused the harm (column 3) and the exact nature of the defect within us that caused the harm and blocked us from God's will (column 4).

Column 1 Who did I harm?	Column 2 What did I do?	Self Column 3 AFFECTS MY (Which part of self caused the harm?)									Column 4 What is the exact nature of my wrongs, faults, mistakes, defects, shortcomings?						
		Social Instinct		Security Instinct		Sex Instinct		Ambitions									
		Self-Esteem	Personal relationships	Material	Emotional	Acceptable sex relations	Hidden Sex relations	Social	Security	Sexual	Selfish	Dishonest	Self-seeking & frightened	Inconsiderate	Being vain and self-promoting	Trying to look good	Being emotionally detached
1																	
2																	
3																	
4																	
5																	
6																	
7																	
8																	

Review of Fears - FOUR

INSTRUCTIONS FOR COMPLETION

1. In dealing with fears, we set them on paper. We listed people, institutions or principle with whom we were fearful (complete column 1 from top to bottom. Do nothing on columns 2, 3 or 4 until column 1 is complete).

2. We asked ourselves why do I have the fear (complete column 2 from top to bottom. Do nothing on columns 3 or 4 until column 2 is complete).

3. Which part of self caused the fear? Was it our self-esteem, our security, our ambitions, our personal or sex relations which had been interfered with? (complete each column within column 3 from top to bottom, starting with the self-esteem column and finishing with the sexual ambitions column. Do nothing on column 4 until column 3 is complete).

4. Referring to our list again, putting out of our minds the wrongs others have done, we resolutely looked for our own mistakes. Where had we been selfish, dishonest, self-seeking and frightened and inconsiderate? (asking ourselves the above questions, we complete column 4).

5. Reading from left to right, we now see the fear (column 1), why do I have the fear (column 2), the part of self that caused the fear (column 3) and the exact nature of the defect within us that allowed the fear to surface and block us from God's will (column 4).

#	**Column 1** I'm fearful of:	**Column 2** Why do I have the fear?	Self — **Column 3** AFFECTS MY (Which part of self caused the fear?)									**Column 4** What is the exact nature of my wrongs, faults, mistakes, defects, shortcomings?						
			Social Instinct		Security Instinct		Sex Instinct		Ambitions			Selfish	Dishonest	Self-seeking & frightened	Inconsiderate	Being envious of others	Getting lost in self-pity	Being self-absorbed
			Self-Esteem	Personal relationships	Material	Emotional	Acceptable sex relations	Hidden Sex relations	Social	Security	Sexual							
1																		
2																		
3																		
4																		
5																		
6																		
7																		
8																		

Review of Resentments – FOUR

INSTRUCTIONS FOR COMPLETION

1. In dealing with resentments, we set them on paper. We listed people, institutions or principles with whom we were angry (completely column 1 from top to bottom. Do nothing on columns 2, 3 or 4 until column 1 is complete).

2. We asked ourselves why we were angry (completely column 2 from top to bottom. Do nothing on columns 3 or 4 until column 2 is complete).

3. On our grudge list we set opposite each name our injuries. Was it our self-esteem, our security, our ambitions, our personal or sex relations which had been interfered with? (complete each column within column 3 from top to bottom, starting with the self-esteem column and finishing with the sexual ambitions column). Do nothing on column 4 until column 3 is complete).

4. Referring to our list again, putting out of our minds the wrongs others have done, we resolutely looked for our own mistakes. Where had we been selfish, dishonest, self-seeking and frightened and inconsiderate? (asking ourselves the above questions, we complete column 4).

5. Reading from left to right, we now see the resentment (column 1), the cause (column 2), the part of self that had been affected (column 3) and the exact nature of the defect within us that allowed the resentment to surface and block us from God's will (column 4).

	Column 1 I'm resentful at:	Column 2 The cause:
1		
2		
3		
4		
5		
6		
7		
8		

Self Column 3 AFFECTS MY (Which part of self is affected?)									Column 4 What is the exact nature of my wrongs, faults, mistakes, defects, shortcomings?							
Social Instinct		Security Instinct		Sex Instinct		Ambitions										
Self-Esteem	Personal relationships	Material	Emotional	Acceptable sex relations	Hidden Sex relations	Social	Security	Sexual	Selfish	Dishonest	Self-seeking & frightened	Inconsiderate	Being envious of others	Getting lost in self-pity	Being self-absorbed

Review of our own sex conduct - FOUR

INSTRUCTIONS FOR COMPLETION

1. We listed all the people we harmed (complete column 1 from top to bottom. Do nothing on columns 2, 3 or 4 until column 1 is complete).
2. We asked ourselves what we did (complete column 2 from top to bottom. Do nothing on columns 3 or 4 until column 2 is complete).
3. Was it our self-esteem, our security, our ambitions, our personal or sex relations that caused the harm? (complete each column within column 3 from top to bottom, starting with the self-esteem column and finishing with the sexual ambitions column. Do nothing on column 4 until column 3 is complete).
4. Referring to our list again, putting out of our minds the wrongs others had done, we resolutely looked for our own mistakes. Where had we been selfish, dishonest, self-seeking and frightened and inconsiderate? (asking ourselves the above questions, we complete column 4).
5. Reading from left to right, we now see the harm (column 1), what we did (column 2), the part of self that caused the harm (column 3) and the exact nature of the defect within us that caused the harm and blocked us from God's will (column 4).

Column 1 Who did I harm?	Column 2 What did I do?	Self Column 3 AFFECTS MY (Which part of self caused the harm?)								Column 4 What is the exact nature of my wrongs, faults, mistakes, defects, shortcomings?							
		Social Instinct		Security Instinct		Sex Instinct		Ambitions									
		Self-Esteem	Personal relationships	Material	Emotional	Acceptable sex relations	Hidden Sex relations	Social	Security	Sexual	Selfish	Dishonest	Self-seeking & frightened	Inconsiderate	Being envious of others	Getting lost in self-pity	Being self-absorbed
1																	
2																	
3																	
4																	
5																	
6																	
7																	
8																	

Review of Fears - FIVE

INSTRUCTIONS FOR COMPLETION

1. In dealing with fears, we set them on paper. We listed people, institutions or principle with whom we were fearful (complete column 1 from top to bottom. Do nothing on columns 2, 3 or 4 until column 1 is complete).

2. We asked ourselves why do I have the fear (complete column 2 from top to bottom. Do nothing on columns 3 or 4 until column 2 is complete).

3. Which part of self caused the fear? Was it our self-esteem, our security, our ambitions, our personal or sex relations which had been interfered with? (complete each column within column 3 from top to bottom, starting with the self-esteem column and finishing with the sexual ambitions column. Do nothing on column 4 until column 3 is complete).

4. Referring to our list again, putting out of our minds the wrongs others have done, we resolutely looked for our own mistakes. Where had we been selfish, dishonest, self-seeking and frightened and inconsiderate? (asking ourselves the above questions, we complete column 4).

5. Reading from left to right, we now see the fear (column 1), why do I have the fear (column 2), the part of self that caused the fear (column 3) and the exact nature of the defect within us that allowed the fear to surface and block us from God's will (column 4).

			Self Column 3 AFFECTS MY (Which part of self caused the fear?)									Column 4						
Column 1 I'm fearful of:	**Column 2** Why do I have the fear?		Social Instinct		Security Instinct		Sex Instinct		Ambitions			What is the exact nature of my wrongs, faults, mistakes, defects, shortcomings?						
			Self-Esteem	Personal relationships	Material	Emotional	Acceptable sex relations	Hidden Sex relations	Social	Security	Sexual	Selfish	Dishonest	Self-seeking & frightened	Inconsiderate	Being emotionally withholding	Trying to live life in the mind	Being Secretive
1																		
2																		
3																		
4																		
5																		
6																		
7																		
8																		

Review of Resentments – FIVE

INSTRUCTIONS FOR COMPLETION

1. In dealing with resentments, we set them on paper. We listed people, institutions or principles with whom we were angry (completely column 1 from top to bottom. Do nothing on columns 2, 3 or 4 until column 1 is complete).

2. We asked ourselves why we were angry (completely column 2 from top to bottom. Do nothing on columns 3 or 4 until column 2 is complete).

3. On our grudge list we set opposite each name our injuries. Was it our self-esteem, our security, our ambitions, our personal or sex relations which had been interfered with? (complete each column within column 3 from top to bottom, starting with the self-esteem column and finishing with the sexual ambitions column). Do nothing on column 4 until column 3 is complete).

4. Referring to our list again, putting out of our minds the wrongs others have done, we resolutely looked for our own mistakes. Where had we been selfish, dishonest, self-seeking and frightened and inconsiderate? (asking ourselves the above questions, we complete column 4).

5. Reading from left to right, we now see the resentment (column 1), the cause (column 2), the part of self that had been affected (column 3) and the exact nature of the defect within us that allowed the resentment to surface and block us from God's will (column 4).

	Column 1 I'm resentful at:	Column 2 The cause:	Self Column 3 AFFECTS MY (Which part of self is affected?)									Column 4 What is the exact nature of my wrongs, faults, mistakes, defects, shortcomings?						
			Social Instinct		Security Instinct		Sex Instinct		Ambitions									
			Self-Esteem	Personal relationships	Material	Emotional	Acceptable sex relations	Hidden Sex relations	Social	Security	Sexual	Selfish	Dishonest	Self-seeking & frightened	Inconsiderate	Being emotionally withholding	Trying to live life in the mind	Being secretive
1																		
2																		
3																		
4																		
5																		
6																		
7																		
8																		

Review of our own sex conduct - FIVE

INSTRUCTIONS FOR COMPLETION

1. We listed all the people we harmed (complete column 1 from top to bottom. Do nothing on columns 2, 3 or 4 until column 1 is complete).

2. We asked ourselves what we did (complete column 2 from top to bottom. Do nothing on columns 3 or 4 until column 2 is complete).

3. Was it our self-esteem, our security, our ambitions, our personal or sex relations that caused the harm? (complete each column within column 3 from top to bottom, starting with the self-esteem column and finishing with the sexual ambitions column. Do nothing on column 4 until column 3 is complete).

4. Referring to our list again, putting out of our minds the wrongs others had done, we resolutely looked for our own mistakes. Where had we been selfish, dishonest, self-seeking and frightened and inconsiderate? (asking ourselves the above questions, we complete column 4).

5. Reading from left to right, we now see the harm (column 1), what we did (column 2), the part of self that caused the harm (column 3) and the exact nature of the defect within us that caused the harm and blocked us from God's will (column 4).

	Column 1 Who did I harm?	Column 2 What did I do?	Self Column 3 AFFECTS MY (Which part of self caused the harm?)										Column 4 What is the exact nature of my wrongs, faults, mistakes, defects, shortcomings?							
			Social Instinct		Security Instinct		Sex Instinct		Ambitions										
			Self-Esteem	Personal relationships	Material	Emotional	Acceptable sex relations	Hidden Sex relations	Social	Security	Sexual	Selfish	Dishonest	Self-seeking & frightened	Inconsiderate	Being emotionally withholding	Trying to live life in the mind	Being secretive
1																		
2																		
3																		
4																		
5																		
6																		
7																		
8																		

Review of Fears - SIX

INSTRUCTIONS FOR COMPLETION

1. In dealing with fears, we set them on paper. We listed people, institutions or principle with whom we were fearful (complete column 1 from top to bottom. Do nothing on columns 2, 3 or 4 until column 1 is complete).

2. We asked ourselves why do I have the fear (complete column 2 from top to bottom. Do nothing on columns 3 or 4 until column 2 is complete).

3. Which part of self caused the fear? Was it our self-esteem, our security, our ambitions, our personal or sex relations which had been interfered with? (complete each column within column 3 from top to bottom, starting with the self-esteem column and finishing with the sexual ambitions column. Do nothing on column 4 until column 3 is complete).

4. Referring to our list again, putting out of our minds the wrongs others have done, we resolutely looked for our own mistakes. Where had we been selfish, dishonest, self-seeking and frightened and inconsiderate? (asking ourselves the above questions, we complete column 4).

5. Reading from left to right, we now see the fear (column 1), why do I have the fear (column 2), the part of self that caused the fear (column 3) and the exact nature of the defect within us that allowed the fear to surface and block us from God's will (column 4).

| | | Self — Column 3 — AFFECTS MY (Which part of self caused the fear?) | | | | | | | | | Column 4 | | | | | | |
| | | Social Instinct | | Security Instinct | | Sex Instinct | | Ambitions | | | | | | | | | |
Column 1 — I'm fearful of:	Column 2 — Why do I have the fear?	Self-Esteem	Personal relationships	Material	Emotional	Acceptable sex relations	Hidden Sex relations	Social	Security	Sexual	Selfish	Dishonest	Self-seeking & frightened	Inconsiderate	Being in worry and doubt	Being anxious or fearful	Being pessimistic
1																	
2																	
3																	
4																	
5																	
6																	
7																	
8																	

Review of Resentments – SIX

INSTRUCTIONS FOR COMPLETION

1. In dealing with resentments, we set them on paper. We listed people, institutions or principles with whom we were angry (completely column 1 from top to bottom. Do nothing on columns 2, 3 or 4 until column 1 is complete).

2. We asked ourselves why we were angry (completely column 2 from top to bottom. Do nothing on columns 3 or 4 until column 2 is complete).

3. On our grudge list we set opposite each name our injuries. Was it our self-esteem, our security, our ambitions, our personal or sex relations which had been interfered with? (complete each column within column 3 from top to bottom, starting with the self-esteem column and finishing with the sexual ambitions column). Do nothing on column 4 until column 3 is complete).

4. Referring to our list again, putting out of our minds the wrongs others have done, we resolutely looked for our own mistakes. Where had we been selfish, dishonest, self-seeking and frightened and inconsiderate? (asking ourselves the above questions, we complete column 4).

5. Reading from left to right, we now see the resentment (column 1), the cause (column 2), the part of self that had been affected (column 3) and the exact nature of the defect within us that allowed the resentment to surface and block us from God's will (column 4).

	Column 1 I'm resentful at:	Column 2 The cause:	Self — Column 3 — AFFECTS MY (Which part of self is affected?)									Column 4 — What is the exact nature of my wrongs, faults, mistakes, defects, shortcomings?						
			Social Instinct	Security Instinct		Sex Instinct		Ambitions			Selfish	Dishonest	Self-seeking & frightened	Inconsiderate	Being in worry or doubt	Being fearful	Being pessimistic
			Self-Esteem	Personal relationships	Material	Emotional	Acceptable sex relations	Hidden Sex relations	Social	Security	Sexual							
1																	
2																	
3																	
4																	
5																	
6																	
7																	
8																	

Review of our own sex conduct - SIX

INSTRUCTIONS FOR COMPLETION

1. We listed all the people we harmed (complete column 1 from top to bottom. Do nothing on columns 2, 3 or 4 until column 1 is complete).

2. We asked ourselves what we did (complete column 2 from top to bottom. Do nothing on columns 3 or 4 until column 2 is complete).

3. Was it our self-esteem, our security, our ambitions, our personal or sex relations that caused the harm? (complete each column within column 3 from top to bottom, starting with the self-esteem column and finishing with the sexual ambitions column. Do nothing on column 4 until column 3 is complete).

4. Referring to our list again, putting out of our minds the wrongs others had done, we resolutely looked for our own mistakes. Where had we been selfish, dishonest, self-seeking and frightened and inconsiderate? (asking ourselves the above questions, we complete column 4).

5. Reading from left to right, we now see the harm (column 1), what we did (column 2), the part of self that caused the harm (column 3) and the exact nature of the defect within us that caused the harm and blocked us from God's will (column 4).

Column 1 Who did I harm?	Column 2 What did I do?	Self — Column 3 AFFECTS MY (Which part of self caused the harm?)								Column 4 What is the exact nature of my wrongs, faults, mistakes, defects, shortcomings?						
		Social Instinct	Security Instinct		Sex Instinct		Ambitions									
		Self-Esteem	Personal relationships	Material	Emotional	Acceptable sex relations	Hidden Sex relations	Social	Security	Sexual	Selfish	Dishonest	Self-seeking & frightened	Inconsiderate	Being in worry or doubt	Being fearful	Being pessimistic
1																	
2																	
3																	
4																	
5																	
6																	
7																	
8																	

Review of Fears - SEVEN

INSTRUCTIONS FOR COMPLETION

1. In dealing with fears, we set them on paper. We listed people, institutions or principle with whom we were fearful (complete column 1 from top to bottom. Do nothing on columns 2, 3 or 4 until column 1 is complete).

2. We asked ourselves why do I have the fear (complete column 2 from top to bottom. Do nothing on columns 3 or 4 until column 2 is complete).

3. Which part of self caused the fear? Was it our self-esteem, our security, our ambitions, our personal or sex relations which had been interfered with? (complete each column within column 3 from top to bottom, starting with the self-esteem column and finishing with the sexual ambitions column. Do nothing on column 4 until column 3 is complete).

4. Referring to our list again, putting out of our minds the wrongs others have done, we resolutely looked for our own mistakes. Where had we been selfish, dishonest, self-seeking and frightened and inconsiderate? (asking ourselves the above questions, we complete column 4).

5. Reading from left to right, we now see the fear (column 1), why do I have the fear (column 2), the part of self that caused the fear (column 3) and the exact nature of the defect within us that allowed the fear to surface and block us from God's will (column 4).

	Column 1 I'm fearful of:	Column 2 Why do I have the fear?	Self Column 3 AFFECTS MY (Which part of self caused the fear?)									Column 4 What is the exact nature of my wrongs, faults, mistakes, defects, shortcomings?							
			Social Instinct	Security Instinct		Sex Instinct		Ambitions										
			Self-Esteem	Personal relationships	Material	Emotional	Acceptable sex relations	Hidden Sex relations	Social	Security	Sexual	Selfish	Dishonest	Self-seeking & frightened	Inconsiderate	Being caught up in the need for intensity	Being caught in planning and anticipation	Being scattered and excessive
1																		
2																		
3																		
4																		
5																		
6																		
7																		
8																		

Review of Resentments – SEVEN

INSTRUCTIONS FOR COMPLETION

1. In dealing with resentments, we set them on paper. We listed people, institutions or principles with whom we were angry (completely column 1 from top to bottom. Do nothing on columns 2, 3 or 4 until column 1 is complete).

2. We asked ourselves why we were angry (completely column 2 from top to bottom. Do nothing on columns 3 or 4 until column 2 is complete).

3. On our grudge list we set opposite each name our injuries. Was it our self-esteem, our security, our ambitions, our personal or sex relations which had been interfered with? (complete each column within column 3 from top to bottom, starting with the self-esteem column and finishing with the sexual ambitions column). Do nothing on column 4 until column 3 is complete).

4. Referring to our list again, putting out of our minds the wrongs others have done, we resolutely looked for our own mistakes. Where had we been selfish, dishonest, self-seeking and frightened and inconsiderate? (asking ourselves the above questions, we complete column 4).

5. Reading from left to right, we now see the resentment (column 1), the cause (column 2), the part of self that had been affected (column 3) and the exact nature of the defect within us that allowed the resentment to surface and block us from God's will (column 4).

	Column 1 I'm resentful at:	Column 2 The cause:	Self Column 3 AFFECTS MY (Which part of self is affected?)								Column 4 What is the exact nature of my wrongs, faults, mistakes, defects, shortcomings?						
			Social Instinct	Security Instinct		Sex Instinct		Ambitions									
			Self-Esteem	Personal relationships	Material	Emotional	Acceptable sex relations	Hidden Sex relations	Social	Security	Sexual	Selfish	Dishonest	Self-seeking & frightened	Inconsiderate	Being caught up in the need for intensity	Being caught in planning and anticipation	Being scattered and excessive
1																		
2																		
3																		
4																		
5																		
6																		
7																		
8																		

Review of our own sex conduct - SEVEN

INSTRUCTIONS FOR COMPLETION

1. We listed all the people we harmed (complete column 1 from top to bottom. Do nothing on columns 2, 3 or 4 until column 1 is complete).
2. We asked ourselves what we did (complete column 2 from top to bottom. Do nothing on columns 3 or 4 until column 2 is complete).
3. Was it our self-esteem, our security, our ambitions, our personal or sex relations that caused the harm? (complete each column within column 3 from top to bottom, starting with the self-esteem column and finishing with the sexual ambitions column. Do nothing on column 4 until column 3 is complete).
4. Referring to our list again, putting out of our minds the wrongs others had done, we resolutely looked for our own mistakes. Where had we been selfish, dishonest, self-seeking and frightened and inconsiderate? (asking ourselves the above questions, we complete column 4).
5. Reading from left to right, we now see the harm (column 1), what we did (column 2), the part of self that caused the harm (column 3) and the exact nature of the defect within us that caused the harm and blocked us from God's will (column 4).

	Column 1 Who did I harm?	Column 2 What did I do?	Self Column 3 AFFECTS MY (Which part of self caused the harm?)									Column 4 What is the exact nature of my wrongs, faults, mistakes, defects, shortcomings?						
			Social Instinct		Security Instinct		Sex Instinct		Ambitions										
			Self-Esteem	Personal relationships	Material	Emotional	Acceptable sex relations	Hidden Sex relations	Social	Security	Sexual	Selfish	Dishonest	Self-seeking & frightened	Inconsiderate	Being caught up in the need for intensity	Being caught in planning and anticipation	Being scattered and excessive
1																		
2																		
3																		
4																		
5																		
6																		
7																		
8																		

Review of Fears - EIGHT

INSTRUCTIONS FOR COMPLETION

1. In dealing with fears, we set them on paper. We listed people, institutions or principle with whom we were fearful (complete column 1 from top to bottom. Do nothing on columns 2, 3 or 4 until column 1 is complete).

2. We asked ourselves why do I have the fear (complete column 2 from top to bottom. Do nothing on columns 3 or 4 until column 2 is complete).

3. Which part of self caused the fear? Was it our self-esteem, our security, our ambitions, our personal or sex relations which had been interfered with? (complete each column within column 3 from top to bottom, starting with the self-esteem column and finishing with the sexual ambitions column. Do nothing on column 4 until column 3 is complete).

4. Referring to our list again, putting out of our minds the wrongs others have done, we resolutely looked for our own mistakes. Where had we been selfish, dishonest, self-seeking and frightened and inconsiderate? (asking ourselves the above questions, we complete column 4).

5. Reading from left to right, we now see the fear (column 1), why do I have the fear (column 2), the part of self that caused the fear (column 3) and the exact nature of self that caused the fear to surface and block us from God's will (column 4).

Column 1 I'm fearful of:	Column 2 Why do I have the fear?	Self Column 3 AFFECTS MY (Which part of self caused the fear?)								Column 4 What is the exact nature of my wrongs, faults, mistakes, defects, shortcomings?						
		Social Instinct	Security Instinct		Sex Instinct		Ambitions									
		Self-Esteem	Personal relationships	Material	Emotional	Acceptable sex relations	Hidden Sex relations	Social	Security	Sexual	Selfish	Dishonest	Self-seeking & frightened	Inconsiderate	Being in lust of power and things	Seeing people as objects	Being dominating and confrontational
1																	
2																	
3																	
4																	
5																	
6																	
7																	
8																	

Review of Resentments – EIGHT

INSTRUCTIONS FOR COMPLETION

1. In dealing with resentments, we set them on paper. We listed people, institutions or principles with whom we were angry (completely column 1 from top to bottom. Do nothing on columns 2, 3 or 4 until column 1 is complete).

2. We asked ourselves why we were angry (completely column 2 from top to bottom. Do nothing on columns 3 or 4 until column 2 is complete).

3. On our grudge list we set opposite each name our injuries. Was it our self-esteem, our security, our ambitions, our personal or sex relations which had been interfered with? (complete each column within column 3 from top to bottom, starting with the self-esteem column and finishing with the sexual ambitions column). Do nothing on column 4 until column 3 is complete).

4. Referring to our list again, putting out of our minds the wrongs others have done, we resolutely looked for our own mistakes. Where had we been selfish, dishonest, self-seeking and frightened and inconsiderate? (asking ourselves the above questions, we complete column 4).

5. Reading from left to right, we now see the resentment (column 1), the cause (column 2), the part of self that had been affected (column 3) and the exact nature of the defect within us that allowed the resentment to surface and block us from God's will (column 4).

	Column 1 I'm resentful at:	Column 2 The cause:	Self Column 3 AFFECTS MY (Which part of self is affected?)									Column 4 What is the exact nature of my wrongs, faults, mistakes, defects, shortcomings?						
			Social Instinct		Security Instinct		Sex Instinct		Ambitions									
			Self-Esteem	Personal relationships	Material	Emotional	Acceptable sex relations	Hidden Sex relations	Social	Security	Sexual	Selfish	Dishonest	Self-seeking & frightened	Inconsiderate	Being in lust of power and things	Seeing people as objects	Being dominating and confrontational
1																		
2																		
3																		
4																		
5																		
6																		
7																		
8																		

Review of our own sex conduct - EIGHT

INSTRUCTIONS FOR COMPLETION

1. We listed all the people we harmed (complete column 1 from top to bottom. Do nothing on columns 2, 3 or 4 until column 1 is complete).

2. We asked ourselves what we did (complete column 2 from top to bottom. Do nothing on columns 3 or 4 until column 2 is complete).

3. Was it our self-esteem, our security, our ambitions, our personal or sex relations that caused the harm? (complete each column within column 3 from top to bottom, starting with the self-esteem column and finishing with the sexual ambitions column. Do nothing on column 4 until column 3 is complete).

4. Referring to our list again, putting out of our minds the wrongs others had done, we resolutely looked for our own mistakes. Where had we been selfish, dishonest, self-seeking and frightened and inconsiderate? (asking ourselves the above questions, we complete column 4).

5. Reading from left to right, we now see the harm (column 1), what we did (column 2), the part of self that caused the harm (column 3) and the exact nature of the defect within us that caused the harm and blocked us from God's will (column 4).

Column 1 Who did I harm?	Column 2 What did I do?	Self Column 3 AFFECTS MY (Which part of self caused the harm?)									Column 4 What is the exact nature of my wrongs, faults, mistakes, defects, shortcomings?							
		Social Instinct		Security Instinct	Sex Instinct		Ambitions											
		Self-Esteem	Personal relationships	Material	Emotional	Acceptable sex relations	Hidden Sex relations	Social	Security	Sexual	Selfish	Dishonest	Self-seeking & frightened	Inconsiderate	Being in lust of power and things	Seeing people as objects	Being dominating and confrontational
1																	
2																	
3																	
4																	
5																	
6																	
7																	
8																	

Review of Fears - NINE

INSTRUCTIONS FOR COMPLETION

1. In dealing with fears, we set them on paper. We listed people, institutions or principle with whom we were fearful (complete column 1 from top to bottom. Do nothing on columns 2, 3 or 4 until column 1 is complete).

2. We asked ourselves why do I have the fear? (complete column 2 from top to bottom. Do nothing on columns 3 or 4 until column 2 is complete).

3. Which part of self caused the fear? Was it our self-esteem, our security, our ambitions, our personal or sex relations which had been interfered with? (complete each column within column 3 from top to bottom, starting with the self-esteem column and finishing with the sexual ambitions column. Do nothing on column 4 until column 3 is complete).

4. Referring to our list again, putting out of our minds the wrongs others have done, we resolutely looked for our own mistakes. Where had we been selfish, dishonest, self-seeking and frightened and inconsiderate? (asking ourselves the above questions, we complete column 4).

5. Reading from left to right, we now see the fear (column 1), why do I have the fear (column 2), the part of self that caused the fear (column 3) and the exact nature of the defect within us that allowed the fear to surface and block us from God's will (column 4).

Column 1 I'm fearful of:	Column 2 Why do I have the fear?	Self Column 3 AFFECTS MY (Which part of self caused the fear?)									Column 4 What is the exact nature of my wrongs, faults, mistakes, defects, shortcomings?							
		Social Instinct		Security Instinct		Sex Instinct		Ambitions										
		Self-Esteem	Personal relationships	Material	Emotional	Acceptable sex relations	Hidden Sex relations	Social	Security	Sexual	Selfish	Dishonest	Self-seeking & frightened	Inconsiderate	Being disengaged from the world	Being stubborn and apathetic	Ruminating or Procrastinating	
1																		
2																		
3																		
4																		
5																		
6																		
7																		
8																		

Review of Resentments – NINE

INSTRUCTIONS FOR COMPLETION

1. In dealing with resentments, we set them on paper. We listed people, institutions or principles with whom we were angry (completely column 1 from top to bottom. Do nothing on columns 2, 3 or 4 until column 1 is complete).

2. We asked ourselves why we were angry (completely column 2 from top to bottom. Do nothing on columns 3 or 4 until column 2 is complete).

3. On our grudge list we set opposite each name our injuries. Was it our self-esteem, our security, our ambitions, our personal or sex relations which had been interfered with? (complete each column within column 3 from top to bottom, starting with the self-esteem column and finishing with the sexual ambitions column). Do nothing on column 4 until column 3 is complete).

4. Referring to our list again, putting out of our minds the wrongs others have done, we resolutely looked for our own mistakes. Where had we been selfish, dishonest, self-seeking and frightened and inconsiderate? (asking ourselves the above questions, we complete column 4).

5. Reading from left to right, we now see the resentment (column 1), the cause (column 2), the part of self that had been affected (column 3) and the exact nature of the defect within us that allowed the resentment to surface and block us from God's will (column 4).

Column 1 I'm resentful at:	Column 2 The cause:	Self Column 3 AFFECTS MY (Which part of self is affected?)									Column 4 What is the exact nature of my wrongs, faults, mistakes, defects, shortcomings?							
		Social Instinct		Security Instinct		Sex Instinct		Ambitions										
		Self-Esteem	Personal relationships	Material	Emotional	Acceptable sex relations	Hidden Sex relations	Social	Security	Sexual	Selfish	Dishonest	Self-seeking & frightened	Inconsiderate	Being disengaged from the world	Being stubborn and apathetic	Ruminating or Procrastinating	
1																		
2																		
3																		
4																		
5																		
6																		
7																		
8																		

Review of our own sex conduct - NINE

INSTRUCTIONS FOR COMPLETION

1. We listed all the people we harmed (complete column 1 from top to bottom. Do nothing on columns 2, 3 or 4 until column 1 is complete).

2. We asked ourselves what we did (complete column 2 from top to bottom. Do nothing on columns 3 or 4 until column 2 is complete).

3. Was it our self-esteem, our security, our ambitions, our personal or sex relations that caused the harm? (complete each column within column 3 from top to bottom, starting with the self-esteem column and finishing with the sexual ambitions column. Do nothing on column 4 until column 3 is complete).

4. Referring to our list again, putting out of our minds the wrongs others had done, we resolutely looked for our own mistakes. Where had we been selfish, dishonest, self-seeking and frightened and inconsiderate? (asking ourselves the above questions, we complete column 4).

5. Reading from left to right, we now see the harm (column 1), what we did (column 2), the part of self that caused the harm (column 3) and the exact nature of the defect within us that caused the harm and blocked us from God's will (column 4).

Column 1 Who did I harm?	Column 2 What did I do?	Self — Column 3 AFFECTS MY (Which part of self caused the harm?)									Column 4 What is the exact nature of my wrongs, faults, mistakes, defects, shortcomings?							
		Social Instinct		Security Instinct		Sex Instinct		Ambitions										
		Self-Esteem	Personal relationships	Material	Emotional	Acceptable sex relations	Hidden Sex relations	Social	Security	Sexual	Selfish	Dishonest	Self-seeking & frightened	Inconsiderate	Being disengaged from the world	Being stubborn and apathetic	Ruminating or Procrastinating
1																	
2																	
3																	
4																	
5																	
6																	
7																	
8																	

84554545R00084

Made in the USA
San Bernardino, CA
08 August 2018